Little Miss Cornbread

Our Journey to Southern-Style Vegan
and Gluten-Free Cuisine
&
Sort-of-True Short Stories

by Susie Jane Wilson and Amylou Wilson

Turtle Lake Press, Fayetteville, AR
Copyright © 2016 by Susie Jane Wilson and Amylou Wilson

All rights reserved. Printed in the United States of America. No part of this book may be used or reproduced in any manner whatsoever without written permission.

ISBN: 978-0-9907229-0-8
Library of Congress Control Number: 2016917812

Editors: Ginny Masullo and Barbara Jaquish
Book and Cover design by Sara Schmidt
Logo design by Sara Schmidt

For Information Contact ⇢
1833 E. Applebury Drive, Fayetteville, Arkansas 72701
www.turtlelakepress.com

Praise for Little Miss Cornbread

As a vegetarian for over forty years, this is the kind of cookbook that might keep families together. Following the vegetarian/vegan recipes with omnivorous versions (plus some extras), provides a cook with some options. And as someone who loves to cook, I love options. These tend toward the kind of meals that fill you up but don't send you directly into that downward spiral toward a nap. I should also mention these are very Southern recipes, something often missing in the vegetarian section of most restaurant menus. The Wilson sisters are fine storytellers, bringing their own enthusiastic and charming tales into these recipes, and Amylou even contributes three fine short stories with themes introduced throughout the cookbook.

So crank up the oven, and while you are waiting on that Spicy Vegan Jalapeno Cornbread to bake, sneak in a little reading.

—Marck L. Beggs, poet and professor.
(And, for what it's worth, a lifetime vegetarian who was voted as one of the top-10 sexiest vegetarians (non-celebrity category) by PETA in 2009.)

Dedication

This book is dedicated to Mama and Daddy. This photo is circa the 1960s in the driveway of our home in Ferriday, Louisiana (Concordia Parish), with our 1966 Pontiac stationwagon.

"To thine own self be true."
— Shakespeare
(Repeated often by Mary Agnes Weed Wilson, beloved mama.)

"Without leaps of imagination, or dreaming, we lose the excitement of possibilities. Dreaming, after all, is a form of planning."
— Gloria Steinem

The Serenity Prayer
"God grant me the serenity to accept
the things I cannot change,
Courage to change the things I can,
And wisdom to know the difference."
— Reinhold Niebuhr
(A plaque of The Serenity Prayer, was always displayed in our home.)

NOTE: "Calling the Dogs" was previously published in Volume 4, 2002, of the *Arkansas Literary Forum*.

Contents

Acknowledgments 1

How to Use This Book 2

Introduction 3

Short Story: Calling the Dogs 7

Vegan & Gluten-Free Recipes 12

    Entrees 13

    Side Dishes 20

    Desserts 30

Short Story: Lee Catherine and Billy Joe Go to the Picture Show 36

Traditional Recipes 42

    Entrees 43

    Side Dishes 50

    Desserts 60

Short Story: Lizards, Spiders and Snakes 66

How-To Section 75

Acknowledgments

We want to thank a few people who played a part in this journey. If we have left anyone out, we sincerely apologize. Books sometimes take years to complete and this one did. That said, we may have forgotten someone. Please know that we are sincerely humbled and grateful to everyone who helped.

So in no special order, we want to thank Ginny Masullo, Rosemary Culbreth, Janet Starr, Joseph Wilson, Drew Wilson, Bruce Wilson, Gary Weidner, Donna Hamilton, Sara Schmidt, Barbara Jaquish, the late Mary Agnes Weed Wilson (Mama), the late Perry Andrew Wilson (Daddy), Granny Wilson (Rosa White Wilson), Papaw Wilson (William Joseph Wilson), Aunt Frankie (Frances Wilson Culbreth Boyd), all the aunts and uncles, our cousins, and all our friends.

We hope you are entertained and eat well because of some of what you find in this book.

By the way, Susie Jane is the mastermind behind the recipes. Amylou wrote the short stories. Take what you need and leave the rest. Have fun!

Changing our eating habits from how we grew up is, indeed, a journey. A recipe is meant to be a starting point only. Susie's adaptations of her family's and Southern roots' recipes is a perfect guidebook for traveling from traditional to vegetarian to vegan. As someone who is primarily a vegetarian, the use of this cookbook gave me new ideas about vegan cooking. I call myself a "flexitarian," meaning I eat primarily vegetarian/vegan with a desire to travel closer to the vegan way. Using Susie's recipes has deliciously taken me closer to that goal.

Susie's How-to Section is helpful to new cooks or to anyone who is new to Southern cooking. She explains the basics, such as How to Make Roux, and the less familiar, like How to Make Macadamia Cream Cheese.

All of the recipes are easily adapted to vegetarian. An added bonus is the traditional recipes that can be prepared for the meat eaters but with organic and free range ingredients.

Now that Susie's book is in your hands, the journey becomes your own. Don't be afraid to adapt your own techniques and ingredients. Happy trails!

— Ginny Masullo, author of *Eating Healthy in the Fast Lane*

Introduction

When we first began the journey of writing this book, a number of things occurred to me. The first thing was that we had actually been writing this book for the past 20 years or so, as my sister and I gathered my family's stories around us and tested and tasted the Southern recipes that we both grew up with in Louisiana and Arkansas and the new ones I was creating to speak to my lifestyle out in Northern California. The second thing that occurred to me was that we had found a way for my mother and my grandmother and all of my aunts and cousin Rosemary (in particular) to speak through us of their place in the kitchen when we gathered at my Granny at Turtle Lake's old farmhouse in Ferriday, Louisiana, to share a meal and spend some time together. (Ferriday is located in northeast Louisiana in the Delta about 10 miles from the Mississippi River and Natchez, Mississippi.)

Susie and Amylou. Sunday best 1965.

I always felt like such a lucky child to have space to run and play, to be surrounded by so many cousins and aunts and uncles to keep us safe and at the same time to have the freedom that you have when you live in a rural area. Our house was surrounded by woods on three sides and a soybean field on the other. There was a bayou at the back of our road that led all the way to my Granny Wilson's back forty. There was a railroad track that we could walk from our house to my Granny's farm pretty easily. My brothers made a habit of it. They would disappear, and my Mama would call down and ask my Granny if she had seen them.

There was a lot to do and we were great at having fun but still staying out of trouble. There were horses to ride and trees to climb and a big old barn where we could play.

Although I did not know this until I was 13 years old, my mama was not always a great Southern cook. When she first married my daddy, she went to my Granny at Turtle Lake and asked her to show her how to cook up all of my daddy's favorite dishes. Slowly but surely my Granny graciously taught her all the basics, from the secrets of Irish stew to baking the perfect spice cookies. There were often so many of us there--aunts, cousins, uncles and Granny and Papaw--that we had to eat in shifts! First, the men ate, then the children. Women ate last (of course). That's how it was done back in those days.

Aunt Frankie's cousin, Susan Wilson Carter, made this painting of the farm at Turtle Lake for Papaw Wilson (her daddy) to hang in his room at the nursing home. It reverted back to her when Papaw passed away.

I was the youngest child and the younger of the two females in our family. The girls were taught how to cook and clean the house. The boys were taught how to hunt and mow the yard. I was put in charge of breads, rice and potatoes from early on. Because of this, cornbread was my realm. It was the first recipe that I modified in my adult life by replacing buttermilk with soy milk and concocting a blend of gluten-free flours to give just the right texture and the feel of traditional cornbread.

During the same time-span that I was focusing on recipes, my sister was busy writing stories based on our childhood. Some are closer to truth than fiction, some of the lines are blurred and where possible she has embellished the truth, as any good Southern girl would do!

As the years progress, the deep fascination I have with participating in a food culture that challenges our perceptions of cuisine, such as vegan and gluten-free, only grows. Living in California, I see options growing daily for people to make these choices easily, as even larger corporate grocery chains are offering healthy products and organic produce at reasonable prices.

I feel our goal in penning this book is to bring the traditional recipes that my mother and grandmother favored alongside the new ones and to tell the stories of our family evolution and connectedness. We aim to represent the sweetness of each dish, its savory components, all maintained to the true flavor of the South. Without that, there's nothing!

— *Susie Jane Wilson*

Like my "little sister" said in her introduction, we've both been busy collecting stories all of our lives. What's most illuminating to me about what she wrote is this: "Some are closer to truth than fiction, some of the lines are blurred and where possible she has embellished the truth, as any good Southern girl would do!" The three stories written by me are not true. They are fiction. However, they are based on the truth in some instances. For example, I remember lizards falling on a man's head at the front door of our home once and my mother chasing the man away. Did this really happen? Hell, I don't know. But it's fun to write it down and make up a story that fits my memory. I like to entertain and make people laugh. And it is very true that down in Louisiana where we grew up—in Ferriday just down the road from rock-and-roll legend Jerry Lee Lewis—those lizards would gather on screen doors, and many fell on my head when I was a child. I don't think I ever got used to it!

Lil' sis and me in Ferriday by the fireplace.

Oh, by the way, Jerry Lee's family liked our dog Barney so much that Barney disappeared from time to time. (This is how I remember it; my brother Bruce says it's true, and I'm sticking by it.) We'd have to go get him back and tell Jerry Lee he could not have Barney. A gargantuan dog, at least to a small girl like me—I'm just shy of 5 feet tall and continue to shrink with age—Barney resembled a big collie dog crossed with a German Shepherd or some such other mythic dog-creature (think Lassie). I loved him like a brother. I remember riding his back like a horse. Is that true? It is to me. And the part about Jerry Lee taking our dog? Well, as I said my brother Bruce confirms that story, so if he says so, it is damn it! I hope the stories make you laugh, reflect and experience joy. They all contain references to food. Of course they do. Food is central to life. Sort of like water. And to be properly nourished, we must have good food, good company, and good stories. I dare anyone to argue with me about that!

— *Amylou Wilson*

Calling the Dogs
by Amylou Wilson

Lee Catherine pulled the towels, rags, socks, jeans, shirts, and underwear out of the washer and put them in the laundry basket. She headed for the back door closest to the clothesline. Carefully, she pushed the screen door open. Carefully, because she didn't want to disturb the mass of green lizards that covered the whole outer side of the door like a blanket.

Sometimes, Lee Catherine felt like she lived in a swamp, always on the lookout for lizards and wolf spiders, snakes, alligators, and alligator gar that live in the murky, muddy end of the lake. She hated swimming in Lake Concordia where the cypress trees got thick, the water turned black, and the Spanish moss covered every limb in sight. For that's where those gar would be lurking in the dark, just waiting to get hold of one of her little legs.

Lee Catherine willed her mind back to the chore at hand and hauled the basket to one end of the long double clothesline. Then she walked to the pump house for the stepladder. She needed it in order to pin the clothes up, for she wasn't yet tall enough to reach the lines. Her mama barely was. Daddy had to set the lines low because Mama was barely five feet tall. And the way it was looking, Lee Catherine thought she'd be lucky to get as big.

Lee Catherine pinned up the towels and rags, then did underwear and socks. She daydreamed about being a nurse on a battleship in World War II. Lee Catherine had lately become enamored with novels about war and movies about war. After picking vegetables in Granny and Papaw's garden on the farm nearby, the whole family would sit around watching old movies and shelling purple-hull peas or snapping green beans. When the news came on, they'd watch the latest reports from Vietnam. It frightened her and she closed her eyes. On the other hand, she'd read *In Cold Blood* by Truman Capote and discovered her tolerance for reality on the page. She was mesmerized. She scoured the *Concordia Sentinel* weekly for true accounts of grizzly crimes, but few national stories made it into the small weekly paper's pages. The *Natchez Democrat*, published six days a week only twelve miles away in a building overlooking the Mississippi River and surrounded by grand plantation homes and tarpaper shanties, wasn't much better.

Lee Catherine felt a powerful need to be useful, to do something important in her life. Her mama encouraged her to study hard. She let her oldest girl know that she didn't have to grow up and be a housewife and have kids to impress her mama. So Lee Catherine dreamed all the time about what she'd be when she grew up. The last thing on earth she wanted was to stay in this little country town and be treated second-class by some redneck, backward stud who thought he hung the moon.

Lee Catherine had made her mind up that she'd go to college. She read books constantly. Sometimes her daddy fussed at her 'cause she'd hide a book under the seat when they went out for a drive in the car on a Sunday afternoon. He didn't think reading and education were bad or anything, but he told her not to bring the book and then she did, so he yelled at her for disobeying him. Lee Catherine didn't care. She hated being under a man's thumb, even if it was just her daddy's and she was only twelve years old. Nope, Lee Catherine had plans, and nobody, including her daddy, would stand in her way.

She gazed at the soybean fields behind the house, but instead she saw the sea and a ship and wounded men from battle being carried aboard. She replayed a scene from some war movie she saw the night before.

"Lee Catherine, telephone," her mother yelled from a window in the house.

Lee Catherine ran into the house scattering green lizards everywhere, with a couple making it into the den.

"Hello?"

"Hey. It's Mary. What're you doing?"

"I was just hanging out clothes. What are you doing?"

"I was just thinking of riding my bike over. Me and you could go ride by the new kids' house three roads over. Susie Jane says there's an older boy she saw and he was f-i-n-e fine," Mary said dreamily.

"Sure! Let's go. I just gotta finish hangin' the wash. I'm down to the boys' underwear. Yuk! Anyway, let me ask Mama." When she came back to the telephone, plans had changed and her voice sounded mysterious. "I can't go right now," Lee Catherine said. "Mama and I are going shopping. She's getting ready to go right now. And it's not your usual groceries or clothes, either. I don't know what it is, but she sounds funny. I'll call you later."

"Well, what do you think is going on?"

"I don't know. Mama didn't say. She just told me she wanted me to go and that it was something important. Daddy's gone this weekend. He's working a construction job somewhere in Tennessee and it's too far for him to come home just for the weekend. Mama doesn't usually buy anything big without Daddy around."

"Well, call me later and tell me what you got," Mary said, and they hung up.

Lee Catherine, her six-year-old baby sister, Mags, and their determined mother got into the Pontiac station wagon and headed for downtown Ferriday. They lived about three miles from the center of town, so it didn't take long to get there.

Mama parked in front of the Western Auto store, and the girls followed her inside. She headed straight for the appliances.

"Well, girls. What do you think? Is this a good-looking dryer?"

"A dryer! Wow, Mama, we're going to buy a dryer, really?"

"That's right. We're buying a dryer. I've hung my last load, and you have too. It's high time we had a dryer, and I've saved out money from working part-time at the bank to pay for it."

"Afternoon, Miss Louise."

"Hello, Mr. Holloway. I'm looking to buy a dryer today. But I have to be sure it's a good price. I mean, the best deal I can get between here and Natchez. This is the first place I've looked though. Is this a good buy? I need something heavy-duty and reliable. We wash a whole lot at our house, what with John's work clothes and the two boys to keep up with."

"That one there is a good one. That's the very same one me and Alice have at home. And you can't beat the price. I could sell it to you and deliver it this afternoon."

"This afternoon, that soon. Well, let me see. Hmm, I guess that'd be just fine. But, well what if John comes home next weekend and he decides he could beat the price I paid. Not that he will, mind you, but it's a possibility."

"I know what you're getting at Miss Louise. I guarantee you John won't find a better dryer at a better price than this one. If he does, I'll take this one back and give you a full refund. You've got my word."

Lee Catherine looked at her mother, who thanked Mr. Holloway and told him to deliver it any time after three o'clock. First, they had some grocery shopping to do. Lee Catherine started screaming "no more hanging out wash" and did a cartwheel on the sidewalk as they left. Mags screamed and tried to do a cartwheel too, but all she managed was to roll over on her butt.

When Daddy got home that Friday after being gone for three weeks straight, he had a fit. By this time, Mama and the girls had gotten real used to having the dryer. When he yelled at Mama, she just stared at him and didn't say anything.

Daddy spent Saturday morning shopping for a dryer. First he drove east 10 miles to Vidalia and across the Mississippi River to Natchez. After comparing prices on dryers at a few stores, he drove back through Ferriday and gunned it a good half hour north toward Monroe, but all he saw was a lost dog out of the corner of his eye by the woods. So he lit another Winston and turned the truck around.

He pulled his white Chevy into the driveway, scattering gravel into the yard. Barney, a large shepherd-collie mix nearing three years old, ran up to the door wagging his tail. Lee Catherine ran out the back screen door and met her daddy, patties in hand. Her oldest brother, John Jr., had the one side of the double barbecue pit ready to go. It was built from red bricks and tile his daddy had laid himself, the covers on each side of the pit made from cutting a barrel in half. John lit another cigarette, grilled burgers, and demonstrated his ability to blow smoke rings and mingle them with the smoke from the fragrant deer meat as it sizzled on the large grill.

Mama finished patting out the rest of the venison burgers. Mags had a kitchen chair pulled up to the sink so she could reach the faucet and wash the ripe tomatoes from Granny's garden. Lee Catherine's tongue moved across her lips while she concentrated on slicing the tomatoes just right, not too thin and not too thick.

While Daddy finished grilling the burgers and warmed the buns on the hot grill, the girls pulled the last of their father's hot, vaguely pungent cement-spattered khakis and work shirts out of the dryer. From the woods nearby came the sounds of make-believe battle. Ben and a bunch of boys from the neighborhood had a few more minutes to play until they'd hear mamas hollering for them to get on home for supper. Barney brought up the rear when all the boys carrying wooden swords and other homemade weapons scattered from the woods. The hunting beagles followed, King and Queenie leading the pack. Daddy started his dog holler to gather them in and corral them into their pen that fronted the soybean field behind their house. As his voice climbed higher and louder, Lee Catherine and Mags sang along. "H-e-r-e p—u—p—p—y, h-e-r-e p—u—p—p—y, h-e-r-e p—u—p—p—y. H-e-r-e p—u—p—p—y, h-e-r-e p—u—p—p—y, h-e-r-e p—u—p—p—y."

Later that night, after Lee Catherine and Mags were lulled to sleep by the sound of the crickets and the occasional hooting of an owl, Mama got a head start on ironing Daddy's clothes for the long drive up to Cleveland, Tennessee, northeast of Chattanooga on Sunday afternoon. He was foreman of a construction and maintenance crew working on the paper mill there. Daddy was home, and they were safe. After highballs and no talk, Mama and Daddy went to bed. Daddy never mentioned the dryer again.

Vegan & Gluten-Free Recipes

Entrees

Red Beans and Rice Are Nice 13
Baked Tofu with Mushrooms in Foil 14
Vegan Second Line Jambalaya 15
Vegan Mama's Irish Stew 16
Carmen's Famous Vegan Gumbo 17
Lulu's Lost Vegan Chili 18
Southern Vegan Medley Soup 19

Side Dishes

Ferriday Fresh Fried Vegan Corn 20
Fancy Potato and Soy Cheese Casserole 21
Mama's Mashed Vegan Potatoes 22
Mama's Vegan Macaroni and Cheese 23
Holiday Vegan Sweet Potato Casserole 24
Susie's Vegan Cornbread 25
Vegan Waffle Cornbread 26
Spicy Vegan Jalapeno Cornbread 27
Mama's Vegan Irish Potato Salad 28
Notes 29

Desserts

Sister Loves Vegan Chocolate-Banana Pie 30
Perfect Vegan Pumpkin Pie 31
Granny's Vegan & Gluten-Free Turtle Lake Spice Cookies 32
Perfect Vegan Pecan Banana Pie 33
Show-Off Vegan Cheesecake 34
Notes 35

Recipe: RED BEANS AND RICE ARE NICE

Serves: 10

Ingredients

- 3 cups dry kidney beans
- ½ cup diced yellow onion
- 2 cloves minced garlic
- ½ cup chopped green onions
- 1 cup chopped celery
- ¼ cup chopped celery greens
- 1 cup smoked baked tofu (cut into ¼-inch cubes)
- 2 tablespoons dark miso
- 1 teaspoon tamari (similar to soy sauce)
- ⅛ teaspoon sea salt
- ¼ teaspoon cayenne pepper
- ⅛ teaspoon ground black pepper
- ⅛ teaspoon red pepper flakes
- ⅛ teaspoon celery salt
- 1 teaspoon hot sauce
- 3 cups water
- 2 cups cooked brown rice

> SEE "HOW-TO SECTION" FOR INSTRUCTIONS ON PREPARING BEANS AND ON COOKING RICE. I SUGGEST YOU COOK THE RICE DURING THE LAST 40 MINUTES WHEN YOUR BEANS ARE COOKING.

Directions

Put the newly washed soaked beans back into the pot or crockpot and add all other ingredients. I like to cut up my vegetables all at one time and then add them all at once with the tofu, miso and the spices. Fill pot up to 1-inch from the top again with water, approximately three cups.

My favorite way to make this is using a crockpot. If using a crockpot, cook on low heat or high heat depending on your preference and turn down to warm when done, which should be 2 hours if on high and 6 hours if on low heat setting. If on stove top, start on medium high and bring to a boil. Turn down slightly and let beans cook for 1 to 2 hours on medium high boil. Stir often and watch the beans so that they do not run out of liquid or get stuck on the bottom of the pot. Add more water if needed, and add spices again near the end of cooking, if lots of water was added.

Serve this over a generous portion of brown rice. This is best paired with Susie's Vegan Cornbread (recipe on page 25).

SUSIE'S NOTE

Miso is a great aspect of this dish and adds richness often associated with the rich stews and casseroles of Southern cuisine. Garnish with hot sauce of your choice. I like a good Louisiana-style hot sauce. Crystal Hot Sauce is one of my favorites. I prefer more vinegar in the ones I use, but lots of folks love the hot, hot, hot ones!

Recipe: BAKED TOFU WITH MUSHROOMS IN FOIL

Serves: 6

Ingredients

- 3 cups cooked brown rice
- 3 pounds extra firm nigari tofu
- 1 cup tamari
- 3 cups sliced mushrooms
- ½ cup medium chopped raw, sweet yellow onion
- 2 cloves minced garlic
- ½ cup white rice flour
- 5 tablespoons ground ginger
- ½ teaspoon sea salt
- 1 teaspoon ground black pepper
- 4 tablespoons olive oil
- 2 tablespoons vegan margarine
- ½ cup Chardonnay wine or broth
- 1 cup vegan sour cream
- 25 foot aluminum foil

SEE "HOW-TO SECTION" FOR HOW TO COOK RICE

Directions

This recipe requires two iron skillets. Use a 6-inch iron skillet to sauté up the mushrooms, onion and garlic, and a 9-inch iron skillet to brown the tofu. It also requires cooked rice, so I do that first while I am cutting up the vegetables.

Rinse and dry tofu and cut into 3-by-3-inch triangles. Place the tofu slices in a glass pan or plastic container. Lay the slices out flat and then pierce with a fork 3 times on each slice of tofu. Pour 1 cup of tamari over the slices. Cover and refrigerate for 30 minutes.

Slice mushrooms, onions and garlic and set aside in separate bowls.

In a small glass bowl, combine the white rice flour and ground ginger with just a little bit of salt and black pepper. Mix the dry ingredients until the ginger is well mixed into the flour then set aside.

Heat the skillets over medium heat. In one of them, place the 2 tablespoons of olive oil, and in the other place the margarine. When the margarine melts and is getting hot, add the garlic and the mushrooms. Cover and let sizzle for 5 minutes then add the Chardonnay or broth to the mushrooms. Stir gently and let mixture come up to a bubbly boil then reduce heat to medium low and cook covered, stirring occasionally for 10 to 15 additional minutes or until liquid is reduced almost completely. When done, turn off heat and leave in skillet and set aside.

Take the tofu out of the fridge and remove from marinade. Pat dry again, and coat with the rice flour and ginger mixture. Gently place the tofu pieces into the skillet with 2 tablespoons olive oil and the sesame oil. Let tofu pieces brown for 5 minutes. Turn tofu to other side and brown another 5 minutes. Remove tofu slices and set on paper towels to drain.

Heat up the oven to 350 degrees. Make 6 sets of foil pieces by taking 12-by-12-inch pieces of foil and folding them into triangles, once and then once again. Place a piece of tofu in the center of a piece of the foil. Place 1 cup of rice on top of the tofu. Place 1 tablespoon of chopped raw onions on the rice. Place ¼ cup of mushrooms on top of that. Place 3 tablespoons of vegan sour cream on top of that. Bring the edges of the foil together to make it gather in the middle. Repeat this process until 5 of these are made.

Place the 5 tofu-in-foil packets on a cookie sheet. Place in oven and cook for 30-35 minutes. Remove and serve in the foil.

SUSIE'S NOTE

I don't know where Mama came up with this one! It was my first introduction to ginger in the South. She modified it, and then I did as well in replacing the chicken breasts with tofu slices. I have been making this for many years now, and still it is one of the things my friends request the most. Enjoy!

Vegan & Gluten-Free Recipes: Entrees | 15

Recipe: VEGAN SECOND LINE JAMBALAYA
Serves: 10

Ingredients

- 1 cup chopped onion
- ½ cup chopped celery
- 3 cloves minced garlic
- ½ cup chopped red or yellow bell pepper
- ¼ cup chopped green onion
- 2 tablespoons olive oil
- ⅛ teaspoon toasted sesame oil
- 2 teaspoons salt
- 24 ounces baked tofu
- 14.5 ounce can diced tomatoes and juice
- ¼ teaspoon dried leaf thyme
- 1 bay leaf
- ¼ teaspoon cayenne pepper
- ⅛ teaspoon Tabasco sauce
- 1 tablespoon tamari (similar to soy sauce)
- 2 cups uncooked short grain brown rice
- 4 cups vegetable broth

SEE "HOW-TO SECTION" FOR INSTRUCTIONS ON PREPARING BAKED TOFU. IF YOU DON'T PURCHASE THE TOFU ALREADY BAKED.

Directions

Prepare all vegetables by chopping first and keeping in separate bowls. Heat olive oil and sesame oil on medium in large saucepan. Add garlic, onion, celery, red or yellow bell peppers, green onions and pinch of the salt. Sauté vegetables until oil is used up or about 7 minutes.

Add the tomatoes and their juices, baked tofu cut into ½-inch pieces, as well as the remaining salt, thyme, bay leaf, cayenne pepper, Tabasco sauce, tamari, rice and vegetable broth. Bring to a boil and reduce to medium low heat. Simmer it until all liquid is absorbed or approximately 40 minutes.

Remove the bay leaf. Take off of heat and stir before serving. Enjoy!

SUSIE'S NOTE

I often return to New Orleans for either Mardi Gras or the New Orleans Jazz and Heritage Festival annually. Once I met a musician there, toting his "bone" or trombone. He informed me that the Second Line can refer to the people marching behind the musicians. The musicians are the First Line, and the mourners following behind them are the Second Line. The same is true if it is a Mardi Gras parade.

The other meaning of the Second Line is that the dirge or funereal song is the First Line and the happier jazz tune played as the marchers continue on down the street is the Second Line. The First Line is mourning and the Second Line is the celebration of life.

Recipe: VEGAN MAMA'S IRISH STEW

Serves: 10

Ingredients

- 2 cups cooked brown basmati rice
- 2 tablespoons sea salt
- 2 teaspoons fresh ground black pepper
- 1 ½ cups rice flour
- 2 cups baked tofu in 1-inch chunks
- 2 tablespoons olive oil
- 1 cup chopped yellow onion
- 1 clove minced garlic
- 1 teaspoon tamari (similar to soy sauce)
- ¼ teaspoon celery salt
- ¼ teaspoon nutritional yeast
- ¼ teaspoon ground thyme
- 1 whole bay leaf
- 3 cups white or Yukon Gold potatoes (cut into ½-inch pieces)
- 2 cups carrots (cut ¼-inch slices)
- 2 cups celery (cut ¼-inch slices)
- 3 cups vegetable broth
- 1 cup water

SEE "HOW-TO SECTION" TO MAKE BROWN RICE. I SUGGEST YOU PREPARE THE RICE DURING THE LAST 40 MINUTES YOU ARE COOKING.

Directions

Mix ⅛ teaspoon sea salt and ½ teaspoon ground pepper into 1 cup of rice flour. Take the cut-up tofu and roll it in the flour mixture to coat. Heat up 2 tablespoons of olive oil in a cast iron skillet. Get the skillet pretty hot, on medium heat. Add the tofu piece by piece to the skillet. Brown the tofu in the skillet for 8 minutes. Add the onions, garlic, tamari and the spices. Add ½ cup of the vegetable broth and let simmer for 5 minutes.

Move from the skillet to a medium soup pot. Add the potatoes, the carrots, the celery and the rest of the vegetable broth and a pinch of nutritional yeast. Stir gently with a wooden spoon. Bring up to a boil then turn down to medium low and let simmer for 45 minutes or until all veggies are thoroughly cooked and broth is reduced to gravy.

Add up to ½ cup rice flour you used to coat tofu if thickening is needed, and add additional water or vegetable broth if it gets too thick. Stir often to keep from burning bottom. Reduce to warm until serving. Remove bay leaf prior to serving.

Ladle over cooked brown rice. This is great with Spicy Vegan Jalapeno Cornbread (recipe on page 26).

SUSIE'S NOTE

This is a variation on my Mama's homemade Irish Stew. I thought a lot about my Granny Wilson as I created this vegetarian version on a cold San Francisco July day. I have made it for many parties and it's a real hit!

Recipe: CARMEN'S FAMOUS VEGAN GUMBO

Serves: 10

Ingredients

- 3, 12-ounce packages of baked tofu, one each of savory, sesame and teriyaki flavors
- 2 cups chopped celery
- 2 cups chopped yellow onions
- 1 cup chopped green onions
- 9 cloves garlic
- 3 large roasted red bell peppers
- 3 cups okra
- 1 cup rice flour
- 2 teaspoons salt
- 1 teaspoon fresh ground black pepper
- 2 tablespoons olive oil
- 5 tablespoons gumbo filé
- 1 teaspoon cayenne pepper
- 1 teaspoon celery salt
- 32 ounces vegetable broth
- 32 ounces whole peeled tomatoes
- ½ cup Redbridge Beer (or other gluten-free beer)
- 3 cups cooked brown rice

Before you begin, please read about how to roast red peppers with garlic cloves and cook rice, as described in How-to Section, along with making roux.

Additionally, rice should be made 40 minutes before gumbo is ready, and you should mix all dry spices together before preparing this dish. Now, let's begin.

Directions

Cut up tofu into ½-inch squares and set aside. Chop celery, onions, green onions and 3 cloves of garlic, and set aside together. Pull the skins from the roasted red peppers and cut into ½-inch squares and set aside. Chop roasted cloves of garlic into fine pieces and set aside. Cut okra into ¼-inch slices and set aside.

Coat tofu with rice flour (with a bit of salt and pepper added to it). Brown the tofu in skillet for 6 minutes or until golden brown on medium heat together with 2 tablespoons olive oil. Add garlic, onions, and celery into skillet with about half of the spices. Add a little vegetable broth and cover then let veggies "sweat" for 3 to 5 minutes.

In a large stockpot add tomatoes cut up with juice from the can and then add rest of vegetable broth along with all the ingredients from the skillet. Add roasted red peppers, roasted garlic and the rest of the spices. Bring it all to a boil and then turn down to simmer. Add okra and beer. Simmer for several hours to perfection.

Serve over a ¼ cup of rice. Best with cornbread.

SUSIE'S NOTE

Gumbo is the proudest single thing a New Orleans resident can make. So much so, that on any given Saturday or Sunday in a local New Orleans neighborhood, say Gentilly or the Faubourg Marigny, you might find a friendly Gumbo Cook-off Showdown between neighbors sharing balconies or courtyards, the fragrance wafting ever so gently to their other neighbors, resulting in an impromptu Sunday night gathering with music, friends and the resulting gumbo treat!

When I was living there, we had gumbo cook-offs most weekends. We all had our secret ingredients. Mine was Sapporo Beer. I guess any special draft beer will do, but I am partial to Sapporo because it reminds me of a friend in New Orleans who would bring the frosty brown bottles home from work on hot summer days. We would place them in the freezer and take them out to enjoy when they were covered with ice.

Recipe: LULU'S LOST VEGAN CHILI

Serves: 10

Ingredients

- 1 cup black beans
- 3 large roasted red bell peppers
- 6 cloves of garlic to roast with peppers
- 16 ounces baked tofu (savory flavor)
- 1 large yellow onion
- 1 large bunch of celery
- 2 tablespoons olive oil
- 2 cloves garlic
- 16 ounces canned tomato sauce
- 2 tablespoons miso paste
- 2 tablespoons ground cumin
- ¼ teaspoon chili powder
- ¼ teaspoon cayenne pepper
- ¼ teaspoon celery salt
- ½ teaspoon ground pepper
- ½ teaspoon salt
- 32 ounces canned whole tomatoes

SEE "HOW-TO SECTION" FOR INSTRUCTIONS ON PREPARING BEANS AND ROASTING PEPPERS AND GARLIC. PREPARE BOTH IN ADVANCE.

Directions

Cut up the baked tofu into ½-inch chunks, set aside. Cut up the onions to a medium chop, mince garlic and chop the celery into medium to fine slices. Any of the outside tops of celery can be discarded, but the tender tops near the center of the celery can be chopped fine and set aside with the rest of the celery. The tops of the celery will add flavor and texture.

Heat a medium to large skillet with olive oil over medium heat. Add the onions, garlic and celery and then cover. The vegetables will then "sweat" in the skillet for 5 to 10 minutes. In a medium to large stockpot, add sweated vegetables, beans, tomato sauce, tofu, miso and spices. Put the juices from the canned whole tomatoes into the pot. Cut up the whole tomatoes into little pieces and then add to the pot. Lastly, pull the skins from the roasted red bell peppers and then cut the peppers into ½-inch pieces. Add to the stockpot along with the roasted minced garlic. Bring all the ingredients to a boil, then reduce to medium heat stirring often for 45 minutes. Reduce heat to low and continue to cook for 2 hours or until beans are tender and all is combined.

This goes great with Susie's Vegan Cornbread (recipe on page 25).

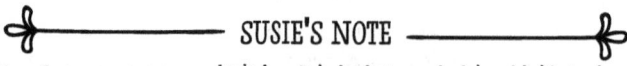

SUSIE'S NOTE

Sometimes I eat vegan just to eat a bit lighter. Baked tofu is wonderful and holds its shape when cut into pieces in the dish. It can be found in most grocery stores under many different brands.

Recipe: SOUTHERN VEGAN MEDLEY SOUP

Serves: 10

Ingredients

- 32 ounces canned tomatoes
- 2 cups carrots
- 3 cups potatoes
- 1 ½ cups chopped celery and greens
- 1 ½ cups chopped yellow onion
- 1 cup diced green onions
- 3 cloves garlic
- 6 ounces canned corn
- 1 cup vegetable broth
- ½ teaspoon sea salt
- ¼ teaspoon cayenne
- 1 teaspoon celery salt
- 1 teaspoon ground black pepper
- 1 teaspoon nutritional yeast
- 1 tablespoon tamari
- 1 dash toasted sesame oil
- 2 teaspoons Crystal hot sauce

Directions

This recipe is easiest if you cut up all vegetables before you begin. It may be made in a large stockpot on the stove or in a crockpot. Begin by putting canned tomatoes, which are cut up, into the pot along with all the tomato juices from the can. Cut the carrots, potatoes, celery, onions, garlic and green onions into ½-inch pieces. Add all the cut-up vegetables bit by bit. Add the vegetable broth. Add the canned corn. Add all spices. Add the tamari, sesame oil and hot sauce.

Bring to boil, or if in crockpot set on high or low, depending on schedule. Reduce heat and cover. If on stove set to medium heat and monitor, as the soup cooks into goodness by an hour or so.

This vegan soup is best enjoyed with Susie's Vegan Cornbread (recipe on page 25).

SUSIE'S NOTE

This vegetarian version of my mama's soup was served quite often. We would have starved to death if it were not for my Granny at Turtle Lake's garden. We ate soups and stews and savory meals all through my youth. At Farmers Markets now I am reminded of the sights and sounds of childhood and home.

✶ End of Entrees ✶

Recipe: FERRIDAY FRESH FRIED VEGAN CORN

Serves: 10

Ingredients

- 15 ears of white or yellow corn on the cob
- 8 ounces soy margarine
- ½ cup white rice flour
- ½ teaspoon sea salt
- ¼ teaspoon black pepper
- 1 cup soy milk creamer

Directions

To cut and dress the corn, follow these instructions. Buy corn on the cob and pull off the husks, and then pull off the silks in the sink. Run water over each corn on cob and get at any remaining silks. You really do not want silks to stay on cob, as they will end up in the skillet too!

Take a corn cob, cut off the knobby end, place the cob on a cutting board, flat cut end down, and run a thin sharp blade down the middle of each row of kernels. Turn the cob and repeat (set aside the juice). After slicing the kernels this way, turn the knife flat and slice the kernels off the corn cob all the way down. This should take about 4 or 5 slices. Set aside with the corn juices and repeat with next cob.

Once you have all your corn set up this way, turn a medium-size skillet on medium heat with 8 ounces of soy margarine in it. Please note if you have any sensitivity to soy, another margarine or coconut oil can be substituted. When the margarine gets so hot it is just about to burn, add the corn. Add the salt and pepper and cover the corn and reduce the heat slightly. Let cook for 4 to 5 minutes, stirring frequently but returning the lid to the pan to get a steaming effect. After 5 minutes or so, add the soy milk creamer slowly while stirring. If you have sensitivity to soy, try almond milk instead as a substitute. Add only as much as needed to keep the mixture going and looking creamy. Cover and watch heat in skillet and keep just below boil.

In a small bowl, mix half a cup of white rice flour with some sea salt and pepper. Open skillet, and add a little of the flour slowly into the liquid. Stir. You only want to use as much of the flour as needed, enough to make the corn thicken up a bit. Cook 3 to 4 minutes more, adding any additional soy creamer if needed. Ferriday Fresh Fried Vegan Corn should be creamy, not sticky. This is so tasty for corn in season.

SUSIE'S NOTE

A simple dish, this is best when the corn is first in season. The smell of this and the sizzle in the skillet tickles the nose with sweetness and reminds me of home.

Recipe: FANCY POTATO AND SOY CHEESE CASSEROLE

Serves: 10

Ingredients

- 3 cups white or Yukon gold potatoes
- 1 ½ cups Sweet Vidalia or yellow onions
- 2 cups soy or nut cheese
- 2 teaspoons olive oil
- ½ teaspoon sea salt
- ½ teaspoon black pepper
- 1 cup soy creamer

Directions

Clean and peel potatoes, and cut into round thin slices. Set aside in a glass bowl with a little water to keep the potatoes from turning brown. Cut onions into ¼-inch pieces, then set aside. Remove cheese from wrapping and crumble or grate into small bits.

Heat oven to 350 degrees. Rub olive oil on inside of a large casserole dish. Place 1 layer of potatoes along the bottom of the dish. On top of this, place a layer of onions and crumbled or grated cheese. Place another layer of potatoes followed by another layer of onions and soy or nut cheese. Continue this process until the whole dish is full or all items are used up. Sprinkle salt and pepper over the casserole. Pour soy creamer into the dish carefully to moisten top to bottom. Cover with any remaining soy or nut cheese.

Place into 350-degree oven and bake for 35 to 40 minutes or until potatoes are fully cooked. Test with fork to see if done, if unsure. Remove from oven, let cool 5 minutes then cut into pieces in the pan to serve. Makes a great side dish just about any time.

Recipe: MAMA'S MASHED VEGAN POTATOES
Serves: 10

Ingredients

- 4 cups red, white or Yukon Gold potatoes
- 6 cups water
- 1 teaspoon sea salt
- 4 ounces soy margarine
- 1 teaspoon fresh ground pepper
- ½ cup soy milk creamer

Directions

First step is to wash and peel potatoes. Cut potatoes into 2-inch chunks. Fill a big glass bowl partially with water to drop potatoes into when cut up. After potatoes are cut, prepare a large stockpot by partially filling it with water.

Drain the potatoes and add them gently to the new water in the stockpot. Add a little of the sea salt to the water. Make sure water in pot covers all of the potatoes. However, make sure pot is not too full, as you do not want it to boil over while cooking.

Place the stockpot with the potatoes and water on the stove on high heat. Bring to boil, then reduce heat to medium and continue to boil while covered, stirring occasionally. Boil until potatoes are tender. You can do a test by removing a potato and sticking a fork into it. This should be about 30 to 40 minutes once it's boiling. If the fork goes through very easily, the potatoes are done. If there is any resistance, potatoes are not done. When done, remove stockpot with potatoes from the stove and drain them into a colander to remove the water.

Place the drained potatoes into a large glass mixing bowl. Add the soy margarine to the potatoes, and let melt partially. Add salt and pepper and a little bit of the soy milk creamer. You can either mix potatoes by hand with a fork or strong whisk or do so with a hand mixer or counter mixer. Add more soy milk creamer as you go. I prefer the hand mixer for this dish, as I like it to be extra smooth.

Coconut oil or canola margarine can be substituted for soy margarine, if you are soy sensitive. Almond milk or coconut milk can be used instead of soy milk creamer as a substitute as well.

SUSIE'S NOTE

I make this for my friends and family. Even if I have just one friend who cannot tolerate dairy products, I don't tell the others that the dish does not have any butter or milk. I love to do this so the person dining with us can eat everything and the others cannot even taste the difference.

Recipe: MAMA'S VEGAN MACARONI AND CHEESE

Serves: 8 to 10

Ingredients

- 4 cups water
- ½ teaspoon sea salt
- 7 ounces thin, gluten-free pasta
- ¼ teaspoon olive oil
- 2 tablespoons soy margarine
- 2 cups nut or soy cheese, sharp cheddar
- ¼ teaspoon fresh ground black pepper
- 2 cups soy milk

Directions

Preheat oven to 350-degrees. In a medium stockpot, bring water and a pinch of salt to boil. Add all of the gluten-free pasta and carefully stir into water. Continue to boil, but reduce heat a little bit and keep an eye on the pot so it does not boil over. Add the olive oil. Stir the noodles as they cook. Boil for no less than 5 minutes and no more than 10 minutes. Pasta should slide off of fork and be tender but be al dente or barely done.

Remove from heat and drain pasta through a colander, removing all water possible. Let it drain for 2 or 3 minutes, but no more.

In a large bowl, place margarine. Add gluten-free pasta to the bowl with the margarine and toss it thoroughly so that pasta moves freely and is not sticky.

Pour pasta into a large rectangular, oven-safe glass casserole dish. Add ½-inch chunks of vegan cheddar cheese to the pasta, along with the rest of the salt and pepper. Toss well within the dish so that cheese is inside and within as well as on top of mixture. Add soy milk to dish and toss slightly. Feel free to substitute canola margarine or coconut oil if you are sensitive to soy products.

Put casserole uncovered into 350-degree oven. Cook for 30-35 minutes.

Remove from oven and let sit for 5 minutes before serving.

SUSIE'S NOTE

The thing about making great tasting vegan dishes is the taste and style of the ingredients. I suggest a visit to your local health food store to look into either nut cheeses or soy cheese. Both are available in sharp cheddar. The choice is yours on how much soy you want in the dish. It's really nice to have a result so thick and creamy, but also gluten-free and dairy-free!

Recipe: HOLIDAY VEGAN SWEET POTATO CASSEROLE

Serves: 10

Ingredients

- 1 tablespoon soy margarine
- 3 cups sweet potatoes or yams
- ¼ cup molasses
- ½ teaspoon nutmeg
- ⅛ teaspoon salt
- ½ teaspoon cinnamon
- 2 tablespoons dark brown sugar
- 1 cup water

Directions

Grease a 9" x 13" glass baking pan with 1 tablespoon of soy margarine.

Preheat oven to 350 degrees.

Peel (or leave skins on) and slice the sweet potatoes, making center-cut pieces or large chunks. The slices should be uniform, about ⅛-inch thick slices. Place potatoes into the casserole dish. (For fun, stack and splay potatoes out like a deck of cards if they are center-cut.) Do so until all potatoes are used up and casserole is full.

Pour molasses over potatoes slowly, covering them all. In a small dish or bowl, mix nutmeg, salt and cinnamon. Sprinkle mixture over the top of the casserole. Crumble a small amount of dark brown sugar over the casserole as evenly as possible. Add enough water to come to ¼-inch from the top of the dish.

Place pan into the 350-degree oven for 30-40 minutes or until sweet potatoes are tender. Check the dish occasionally while cooking and add additional water if the dish becomes dry. You should still have a bit of moisture at the end of cooking time. Remove from oven when done and let cool for at least 5 minutes before serving.

SUSIE'S NOTE

You may want to use honey in place of the molasses. The result with either is rich, thick and brown and makes the sweet potatoes so sweet and tasty that you will not miss the extra brown sugar present in the "traditional" dish. Both are fairly healthy nutritious sugars that are yummy and fun to use!

Recipe: SUSIE'S VEGAN CORNBREAD

Serves: 8 to 10

Ingredients

- 3 tablespoons corn oil
- 2 cups finely ground cornmeal
- ½ cup soy flour
- ½ cup white rice flour
- 4 teaspoons baking powder
- ¼ teaspoon salt
- ½ cup unripe bananas
- 1 ½ cups plain soy milk

Directions

Begin by heating oven to 425 degrees. When oven is heated pour 2 tablespoons of corn oil into a 9-inch cast iron skillet and place the skillet in the hot oven for 10 to 15 minutes or until very hot.

Place a sifter of some kind over a large bowl. Measure out the cornmeal into the sifter then add the soy flour, the white rice flour, the baking powder, and the salt. Sift all ingredients into the big bowl. Make sure all of these dry ingredients are well mixed.

Next, peel the unripe bananas and mash them well. Remove the sifter device and add the bananas and half of the soy milk (sometimes I use soy creamer instead for extra richness). Begin mixing this together with a hand whisk. Add more of the soy milk as needed to make a batter of consistency of cake batter. Add the other 1 tablespoon of corn oil.

Carefully, remove the skillet from the oven. Pour half of the hot corn oil from the skillet into the batter. Mix into batter lightly with fork. Pour batter into skillet and put into oven for 25 minutes or until top of cornbread is golden brown. Check before 25 minutes is up. Remove from oven and turn cornbread out onto a plate. The bottom side should be up and showing.

Let it sit for 5 minutes and then slice like a pie and serve. Slice the "pie pieces" lengthwise and add margarine inside.

SUSIE'S NOTE

I learned to make this cornbread when I was 9 years old. Ever since I became an adult and moved out to California, I have been searching for ways to make great Southern recipes without wheat and most dairy. I enjoy using the unripe banana cut up and mashed as an egg substitute. Unripe bananas are not so sweet but they add texture.

Recipe: VEGAN WAFFLE CORNBREAD

Serves: 5 waffles

Ingredients

- Pam spray
- ½ cup soy cheese cut into ⅛-inch chunks
- ¼ cup finely chopped onions
- ½ cup drained canned corn
- 1 tablespoon minced jalapeno pepper
- 1 large semi-ripe banana
- ½ teaspoon salt
- ½ cup vegetable oil
- 1 cup cornmeal
- ½ cup soy flour
- ½ cup rice flour
- 1 cup soy creamer
- 1 ½ tablespoon baking powder
- 1 tablespoon jalapeno juice

Directions

Begin by cutting up the soy cheese and setting it aside in a small bowl. Next, chop the onions fine and set aside in a small bowl. Then open the canned corn, drain and set aside. Mince the jalapenos and also set them aside. Next, mash the banana until it is almost like a paste. Add in the oil and soy creamer. Sift your cornmeal, soy flour, rice flour, salt and baking powder into the bananas while whisking. Add the soy cheese to the batter and stir it in with a wooden spoon. Add in the onions and the jalapenos, then add in the corn and the jalapeno juice. Stir well with the wooden spoon.

Use a soup ladle to ladle the batter into the waffle iron, covering only half of the bottom griddle. Close and cook on medium high setting until golden brown. Repeat process to make more waffle bread. Serve topped with salsa or green tomato relish.

Recipe: SPICY VEGAN JALAPENO CORNBREAD

Serves: 8 to 10

Ingredients

- 2 cups fine ground cornmeal
- ½ cup soy flour
- ½ cup white rice flour
- 3 tablespoons baking powder
- ¼ teaspoon salt
- 16 ounces soy milk
- ½ cup unripe bananas
- 3 tablespoons corn oil
- 8 ounces canned corn
- 8 ounces diced yellow onion
- 8 ounces soy or nut cheese
- 4 ounces diced jalapeno
- 2 ounces jalapeno juice

Directions

It's best to cut up the onion and jalapeno first and set aside. I also suggest you place 8 ounces of soy or nut cheese in a bowl, as well as the canned corn.

Begin by heating your oven to 425 degrees and placing 2 tablespoons of the corn oil into a 9-inch cast iron skillet. Put skillet into hot oven for least 10 to 15 minutes or until oil is very hot.

Place a sifter over a large glass or stainless steel bowl and add the cornmeal, soy flour and white rice flour, as well as the salt and the baking powder, and sift it all together. Remove sifter and add the bananas and about half of the soy milk, and mix batter together with a whisk. Add the rest of the soy milk to form a fairly thick batter. If the batter seems too dry add a bit more soy milk. Add the canned corn, diced yellow onion, diced jalapeno and the jalapeno juice. Mix well by hand with a fork, and then add the soy or nut cheese by crumbling it into the mix, and stir lightly.

With a nice thick oven mitt, take the skillet out of the oven and pour most of the excess oil in the skillet into the batter. Mix in lightly with a fork. Place the skillet back on the stove top. Pour the batter into the skillet. Place skillet back into oven.

Bake for 35 minutes or until a knife placed into the cornbread comes out clean. Remove cornbread from oven and turn it over on to a plate. Cut into pie-like pieces and share with family or friends.

Recipe: MAMA'S VEGAN IRISH POTATO SALAD

Serves: 10

Ingredients

- 6 cups water
- 4 cups small red potatoes
- 1 cup yellow onion or Maui Onion or Sweet Vidalia onion
- ½ cup green onions
- 1 cup celery
- ¼ cup red bell pepper
- 2 cups cherry tomatoes
- 1 teaspoon salt
- ½ teaspoon ground black peppe
- ½ teaspoon celery salt
- 3 teaspoons tamari
- ½ cup vegan mayonnaise
- 1 teaspoon brown mustard
- 1 cup soy yogurt

Directions

Rinse potatoes in a colander under cold running water. Remove any eyes or dirt. Cut potatoes into 1-inch pieces while leaving the skin on the potatoes.

Place the potatoes into a large stockpot and cover with approximately 5 cups of cool water or to within 1-inch from the top of the pot. Place pot on stove on medium high heat or until it comes to a boil, then turn down slightly and boil potatoes for 45 minutes or until fork goes into potato easily. Remove potatoes from heat and drain in a colander over the sink. Let potatoes sit and cool for 30 minutes.

Place cooled potatoes into a large glass bowl. Rinse and chop the yellow onions, green onions, celery, and red bell pepper into ½-inch pieces. Rinse cherry tomatoes. Pour vegetables into glass bowl with potatoes and cherry tomatoes. Add all of the spices, tamari, vegan mayonnaise, brown mustard and soy yogurt. Stir slowly and carefully with a wooden spoon. Put mixture into the fridge and it will be ready to eat in 6 hours. You can substitute a non-soy yogurt product if you or one of your diners are sensitive to soy.

SUSIE'S NOTE

My sister Amy and I made this fabulous healthier version of our famous Irish Potato Salad one year for the family holiday feast. No one knew there was soy yogurt instead of sour cream or vegan mayonnaise in the mix. This is great for folks who, for whatever reason, have taken dairy out of their diet.

✶ End of Side Dishes ✶

Recipe Notes:

Recipe: SISTER LOVES VEGAN CHOCOLATE-BANANA PIE Serves: 8 to 10

Crust Ingredients

- ½ cup soy margarine
- ¼ cup raw granulated sugar
- 2 cups roasted almonds
- 1 cup powdered sugar

> SEE "HOW-TO SECTION" FOR INSTRUCTIONS ON ROASTING AND GRINDING ALMONDS.

Filling Ingredients

- ⅓ cup white rice flour
- 6 tablespoons raw granulated sugar
- ¼ teaspoon sea salt
- 2 1-ounce squares unsweetened chocolate
- 2 cups soy milk
- 2 tablespoons soy margarine
- 1 cup unripe bananas
- 1 teaspoon vanilla extract

Directions for Crust:

Preheat oven to 350 degrees.

To prepare the crust, begin by greasing a pie plate with soy margarine. Add 2 tablespoons of the raw granulated sugar into the greased pie plate and rotate the pan until it is completely coated. Turn the plate over sink so that any excess sugar from the pie plate falls off.

In a medium glass bowl, combine the finely ground roasted almonds and the powdered sugar. Mix well. Add softened margarine and form into a kind of dough. Add the mixture to the pie plate and form the crust as you go. It should look and perform like a graham cracker crust.

Bake the crust for 10 minutes at 350 degrees. Take crust out and let it cool for at least 30 minutes before adding the pie filling and baking the pie.

Directions for Filling:

Mix flour, sugar and salt. Melt chocolate in soy milk in a double boiler until milk is scalded. Gradually add to the sugar and flour mixture and cook over moderate heat. Stir constantly until mixture thickens and boils. Cook for 2 additional minutes. Remove from heat. Let cool.

In a small separate bowl, mash the bananas. Add soy margarine and vanilla and stir. Let cool.

Combine with the cooled ingredients in the double boiler.

Place filling in the cooled almond pie crust and bake in 350-degree oven for 15 minutes. Take out and let cool on a wire rack until room temperature. Refrigerate overnight and enjoy!

SUSIE'S NOTE

To make this vegan version as yummy as the original took some work. My sister's chocolate pie is a force to be reckoned with, but through tender time and dedication, I concocted the above confectionary treat for those who wish to abstain from dairy. Unripe bananas are not very sweet so the idea is that the chocolate flavor will come through and the banana taste will not overpower the recipe. Try it yourself and see if you like it!

Recipe: PERFECT VEGAN PUMPKIN PIE

Serves: 8 to 10

Crust Ingredients

- ½ cup soy margarine
- ¼ cup raw granulated sugar
- 2 cups roasted almonds
- 1 cup powdered sugar

SEE "HOW-TO SECTION" FOR INSTRUCTIONS ON ROASTING AND GRINDING ALMONDS.

Filling Ingredients

- ¾ cup maple syrup
- ½ teaspoon vanilla
- 1 ¼ teaspoons ground cinnamon
- ½ teaspoon sea salt
- ¼ teaspoon ground ginger
- ⅛ teaspoon ground nutmeg
- 15 ounces pumpkin puree
- 1 ¼ cup soy milk
- ½ cup unripe bananas

Directions for Crust:

Preheat oven to 350 degrees.

To prepare the crust, begin by greasing a pie plate with soy margarine. Add 2 tablespoons of the raw granulated sugar into the greased pie plate and rotate the pan until it is completely coated. Turn the plate over sink so that any excess sugar from the pie plate falls off.

In a medium glass bowl, combine the finely ground roasted almonds and the powdered sugar. Mix well. Add softened margarine and form into a kind of dough. Add the mixture to the pie plate and form the crust as you go. It should look and perform like a graham cracker crust.

Bake the crust for 10 minutes at 350 degrees. Take crust out and let it cool for at least 30 minutes before adding the pie filling and baking the pie.

Directions for Filling:

Preheat oven to 425 degrees.

To prepare the filling, you will need a large bowl. In the bottom of the large bowl, place maple syrup, vanilla, cinnamon, salt, ginger and nutmeg. In a small separate bowl, mash the bananas. Add pumpkin puree, soy milk, and bananas to large bowl, then whisk until well blended. Pour mixture into the baked almond pie crust.

Set pie on the bottom rack of oven. Bake for 15 minutes, then reduce heat to 350 degrees and continue baking for another 45 minutes or until knife inserted into the middle comes out clean. Set pie on a rack and let it cool for 2 hours. Refrigerate pie overnight and then serve.

SUSIE'S NOTE

In the filling, you may replace soy milk with almond milk or coconut milk. In the pie crust, you may want to replace soy margarine with other vegan margarines if you or your diners are sensitive to soy. I have served this to crowds of folks who never knew this had soy milk and no wheat. They thought it was the original recipe! It's so delicious and guilt-free. This pie is fabulous for potlucks or family gatherings in the summer or fall. Using all organic ingredients really makes this recipe pop. A special maple syrup or vanilla will as well.

Recipe: GRANNY'S VEGAN & GLUTEN-FREE TURTLE LAKE SPICE COOKIES

Makes: 20-24 cookies

Ingredients

- 1 cup softened soy margarine
- ¼ cup ripe bananas
- 1 cup chopped pecans
- 1 cup oatmeal
- 2 cups brown sugar
- 1 teaspoon ground cinnamon
- ½ teaspoon ground cloves
- 2 teaspoons vanilla extract
- ½ teaspoon allspice
- 3 cups of a gluten-free flour mix like Pamela's or King Arthur's
- 4 ½ teaspoons baking powder
- ⅛ teaspoon salt

Directions

Preheat oven to 350 degrees.

Make sure margarine is at room temperature or softened. In a small separate bowl, mash bananas.

In a large bowl, combine bananas, softened margarine, pecans, oatmeal, brown sugar, cinnamon, cloves, vanilla and allspice. Stir with wooden spoon.

In a separate bowl, combine flour, baking powder and salt. Stir until mixed. Pour flour mixture over the other ingredients in the large bowl. Stir again until well incorporated.

Spoon cookies onto a non-stick cookie sheet in 1½-inch blobs. (I use a tablespoon.) Bake at 350 degrees or 375, depending on your oven, for 8 to 10 minutes.

Remove from oven. Then loosen each cookie from bottom of pan with metal spatula. Let cool or eat hot!

— SUSIE'S NOTE —

My Aunt Frankie says there was a secret ingredient Granny always put in. She says it may have been brown liquor Papaw kept under the counter. She added just a dash. I tried a gluten-free version of this and left off the secret ingredient. Thank you to my Aunt Frankie, who knew this recipe by heart and gave it to me late on one hot summer night.

Recipe: PERFECT VEGAN PECAN BANANA PIE

Serves: 8 to 10

Crust Ingredients

- ½ cup soy margarine
- ¼ cup raw granulated sugar
- 2 cups roasted almonds
- 1 cup powdered sugar

SEE "HOW-TO SECTION" FOR INSTRUCTIONS ON ROASTING AND GRINDING ALMONDS.

Filling Ingredients

- 1 cup unripe bananas
- 2 cups pecans (1 ½ cups chopped, ½ cup whole)
- ½ cup maple syrup
- 1 cup organic dark brown sugar
- ½ cup almond milk
- ½ cup coconut flour
- 1 ½ teaspoon vanilla extract
- a pinch of salt

Directions for Crust:

Preheat oven to 350 degrees.

To prepare the crust, begin by greasing a pie plate with soy margarine. Add 2 tablespoons of the raw granulated sugar into the greased pie plate and rotate the pan until it is completely coated. Turn the plate over sink so that any excess sugar from the pie plate falls off.

In a medium glass bowl, combine the finely ground roasted almonds and the powdered sugar. Mix well. Add softened margarine and form into a kind of dough. Add the mixture to the pie plate and form the crust as you go. It should look and perform like a graham cracker crust.

Bake the crust for 10 minutes at 350 degrees. Take crust out and let it cool for at least 30 minutes before adding the pie filling and baking the pie.

Directions for Filling:

For this recipe, it is best to have three glass bowls — a small, a medium and a large one. Place the three bowls on the kitchen counter and proceed.

In the small bowl, mash the bananas. On a large cutting board, chop pecans. Add these to the medium bowl and set aside. In the large bowl, combine maple syrup, brown sugar, almond milk, coconut flour, vanilla and salt, and then stir with wooden spoon. Add the bananas into the large bowl 1/3'rd at a time, stirring with the wooden spoon. Add the chopped pecans to the large bowl and stir in with a large wooden spoon.

Turn out mixture into the cooled pie crust. Dot the top with the ½ cup of whole pecans. Place into preheated 350-degree oven and bake for 30-35 minutes. Remove from oven and place on a wire rack to cool. Cover and refrigerate when cooled.

Recipe: SHOW-OFF VEGAN CHEESECAKE

Serves: 8 to 10

Crust Ingredients

- ½ cup soy margarine
- ¼ cup raw granulated sugar
- 2 cups roasted almonds
- 1 cup powdered sugar

Filling Ingredients

- 32 ounces macadamia cream cheese
- 16 ounces vegan sour cream
- 1 teaspoon vanilla extract
- 1 cup maple syrup
- 16 ounce bar organic dark chocolate (optional)

> SEE "HOW-TO SECTION" FOR INSTRUCTIONS ON ROASTING AND GRINDING ALMONDS.

> SEE "HOW-TO SECTION" FOR INSTRUCTIONS ON MAKING MACADAMIA CREAM CHEESE. THIS MUST BE MADE A FEW DAYS AHEAD OF TIME.

Directions for Crust:

Preheat oven to 350 degrees.

To prepare the crust, begin by greasing a pie plate with soy margarine. Add 2 tablespoons of the raw granulated sugar into the greased pie plate and rotate the pan until it is completely coated. Turn the plate over sink so that any excess sugar from the pie plate falls off.

In a medium glass bowl, combine the finely ground roasted almonds and the powdered sugar. Mix well. Add softened margarine and form into a kind of dough. Add the mixture to the pie plate and form the crust as you go. It should look and perform like a graham cracker crust.

Bake the crust for 10 minutes at 350 degrees. Take crust out and let it cool for at least 30 minutes before adding the cheesecake filling and baking cheese cake.

Directions for Filling:

Preheat oven to 350 degrees.

This recipe works best with one large glass bowl and one small one. Into the large bowl, place macadamia cream cheese, vegan sour cream, vanilla and maple syrup. Mix with a hand mixer or with whisk by hand. If desired, to make it really "show-off," cut dark chocolate into ½-inch chunks and stir into the cheesecake batter. Turn out mixture from large glass bowl into pre-cooked pie crust.

Place into oven at 350 degrees for 30-35 minutes. Remove from oven and cool on wire rack for 15 minutes to almost room temperature. Cover cheesecake and refrigerate overnight. Remove from fridge, cut into pie pieces and serve.

✶ End of Desserts ✶

Recipe Notes:

Lee Catherine and Billy Joe go to the Picture Show

by Amylou Wilson

All week, Lee Catherine and Billy Joe had been planning to meet at the movies on Saturday. They decided first thing, at school on Monday, shortly after meeting each other for the very first time. Love at first sight, Lee Catherine thought to herself smiling.

Billy Joe had just moved to Ferriday, Louisiana, from Enid, Oklahoma, which he described as a hellhole of a place. Billy Joe had a colorful vocabulary, and Lee Catherine decided that was one thing she liked about him. He wasn't afraid to express himself. However, he knew not to talk this way around teachers or parents. Then, he was very polite and respectful. Lee Catherine decided that Billy Joe was a very smart boy. Billy Joe would be going places in life.

Lee Catherine first laid eyes on Billy Joe as he walked into school with his mother. He was tall for a fifth-grader. His hair was strawberry blond, and he had light freckles all over his body, at least what was exposed. He wore black jeans and a black button-down shirt. His sleeves were rolled up. He made an impression. No boys in Ferriday dressed that way.

Lee Catherine followed along behind Billy Joe and his mother as they went to the principal's office to get signed up. Then, she saw him later at the first recess on Monday. He had a stick, and he was drawing something in the dirt with it. His arms looked strong.

Lee Catherine was usually shy around new people, but somehow, this was different. She had never felt like this before, like here's someone I want to know, so I'm going to break out of myself and do something about it. She felt good, but she was scared, too. What if he laughed at her? What if he thought she was a third-grader or something? No, she was in his classroom, so he'd have to know she was eleven years old, or around that.

She decided to walk over close by Billy Joe and sit on the round iron bars that served as a decorative fence of sorts for the school grounds. Then she started balancing on top of the fence, walking it, one foot in front of the other, like she was a trapeze artist in the circus and the bar was her tightrope. She held her tiny arms out to balance. She walked away from Billy Joe and focused on the cotton fields across from the school. Then she pivoted and returned, never falling off. She stared at Billy Joe, who finally looked up from his doodling in the dirt.

"Hey," Billy Joe said, rising up from the ground where he had been squatting.

"Hey yourself," Lee Catherine answered. "I'm Lee Catherine."

"I'm Billy Joe. I just moved here from Enid, Oklahoma. It's a hellhole on earth. This place may not be much better, from what I can tell so far."

"Well, maybe it's better than you think. Maybe you should give it a chance," Lee Catherine said, getting defensive. She jumped off the fence, unaware that she had put her hands on her hips as she was speaking to him.

"You're in my class, aren't you? I seen you, didn't I?" he asked.

"That's 'saw' not 'seen,' and yes, I'm in your class. I saw you drive up to school this morning with your mother. I guess that was your mother. Anyway, you don't look like the other boys here. I like your black clothes. They're like what Jimmy Dean wore in that movie 'Rebel Without a Cause.' You know that movie?"

"Sure. Who don't? I mean, who doesn't? Shit, I really remind you of Jimmy Dean?"

"I wouldn't say such a thing if I didn't mean it. I'm honest and speak my mind. That's what my mama taught me to do. Hey, you want to meet me at the picture show on Saturday? It's the Arcade on Main Street. You can't miss it. It's a triple feature. I don't remember what all is playing, but one of the movies is Psycho and I've never seen it. I've heard it's real scary though, and I'd sure like someone to watch it with me, in case I get scared."

"Sure, I'll meet you, as long as Mama says it's okay. What time does it start?"

It was the last Saturday in August. The year was 1969. The war raged in Vietnam, and the nightly news had begun to feature graphic footage that many people found disturbing. If they weren't worried about a son or brother or father or uncle or cousin, it might be the next-door neighbor's loved one.

And lately, the news also included film of longhaired hippies and anti-war activists. Most recently, there had been reports of a huge music festival called Woodstock where thousands of young people had converged on a farm somewhere in rural New York to hear the latest rock-and-roll and folk musicians, and there was talk of a lot of drugs, too. But there weren't many longhairs in Ferriday. The peace movement was practically non-existent here.

As for music, rumor had it that Paul McCartney of the Beatles was dead. But Lee Catherine's oldest brother John Jr. told Lee Catherine that was a big lie. And it didn't seem to matter what happened anywhere else, anyway, Lee Catherine had observed some time ago. Nothing much changed in Ferriday. So, for the time being, the regular school year had begun the past week as it always did.

Lee Catherine stood in front of the full-length mirror inspecting her eleven-year-old body. For the past two days, she had been on a diet. It only took two days for her to achieve what it took other girls weeks to do, she thought proudly. Lee Catherine would notice a paunch in her belly, and she'd decide to cut back. That meant eating two Brown 'n' Serve rolls at Sunday dinner instead of four and limiting herself to no extra helpings, if she could find the willpower. Soon, her little bulge would disappear, and her tummy would lay flat again.

"I may be tiny, but at least I'm not tiny and fat," Lee Catherine said to herself. She was wearing a pair of flowered shorts that zipped up the back and a shirt that matched. You could barely see the shimmer of light brown hair on her little legs. Her white tennis shoes were new.

"I'm leaving, Lee Catherine," her brother John Jr. yelled. "If you want a ride you better get out here right now!" John Jr. had just turned fifteen and begun to drive.

Today was a normal, hot and humid Saturday, perfect for going to the picture show, where the air conditioners hummed and made the theater feel like the inside of a refrigerator.

"I'm coming," Lee Catherine yelled, running after John Jr. Lee Catherine climbed into the old blue International Harvester Scout, a used model John, their daddy, had bought for the children to drive, as well as for a hunting vehicle.

It was two o'clock when John Jr. dropped Lee Catherine off in front of the Arcade. *Psycho* would begin at two-thirty, but there would be cartoons and previews for other movies in between. And anyway, this would give Lee Catherine and Billy Joe time to buy Red Hots and popcorn and Cokes and find a good place to sit.

Lee Catherine didn't see Billy Joe right away. He had his back to her. He was looking at a poster advertising a movie called *Barbarella*, starring Jane Fonda playing a bad girl from outer space.

"Hey," Lee Catherine said, as she walked up behind him.

"Oh, hey. I didn't see you come in. I'm sorry," Billy Joe said, and he reached out and patted her on the shoulder. Billy Joe was wearing his black jeans and a black short-sleeved shirt. She noticed the muscles in his arms again and resisted the impulse to reach out and touch them.

"You want to get some popcorn or something and find a seat?" Billy Joe asked her.

They walked up to the concession stand, and Lee Catherine ordered Red Hots and a small cherry Coke. "I'll have a large popcorn and a large Coke," Billy Joe said. "Put her stuff with mine. I'm paying," and with that he pulled some dollar bills and change out of his pocket.

"You don't have to do that, Billy Joe. I've got money."

"I want to. You're my date, aren't you?"

Lee Catherine hadn't really thought of meeting Billy Joe at the picture show as a date, but then she'd never been on a date before, so she was inexperienced. "I guess so. We're on a date," she answered, feeling all warm inside all of a sudden and smiling at him.

Lee Catherine decided right then she better stop analyzing everything or she would spoil it. Billy Joe was being nice to her, and she'd just go with it and not worry about it, enjoy her first date, try not to act nervous.

They found a seat about midway down in the middle of the row.

The theater was getting full. *Psycho* hadn't played in Ferriday for several years and entertainment of any kind was a big draw around here. There wasn't much else to do but go the picture show or cruise the Sandwich Bar drive-in by the high school, that is if you were old enough to drive.

Lee Catherine's mouth and lips were stained with red, and her breath was as sweet as cinnamon. She screamed and squirmed and closed her eyes during scary parts of the movie. Billy Joe put his arm around her shoulders. When the picture show got real dark, she felt his other arm come around in front of her and land on her shoulder. Then, slowly, he moved his face in front of hers, and she felt his breath on her eyes. He kissed her right eye, then her left one, then moved his lips down to her nose and then to her mouth. He tasted sweet and hot. He put his tongue inside her mouth, and Lee Catherine found herself giving him hers.

Mostly, they missed the rest of the movie then. They kissed every time the picture show got very dark, and Billy Joe held her hand some. Then, he put his other hand on her shoulder again, and before she knew it, he was moving his hand down the front of her shirt. Lee Catherine did not try to stop him. She figured that if he liked doing that, it was okay. It felt good to her, and if he didn't mind how small she was, then she was going to be happy for that. She didn't really have breasts yet, and worried she might never grow any.

Psycho ended and the lights went up for about five minutes. Then there was a cartoon, and a movie about moonshiners came on. Lee Catherine whispered to Billy Joe that he was a real good kisser. She even told him he was the first boy ever to French kiss her.

They spent the whole afternoon at the movies. Back at school, Lee Catherine and Billy Joe would go off to the end of the playground every chance they got and hang out by a tree that concealed them enough so they could kiss some. On Saturdays, they'd meet by the railroad tracks between her house and her grandmother's farm. They'd ride their bikes there and crawfish some between holding hands and kissing. After a few Saturdays of that, Billy Joe suggested they check out a trail in the woods. They went a little ways until they found a clearing under a big oak tree. Billy Joe began unbuttoning his black shirt. Underneath it he had on a white tee shirt with a sexy V-neck. He draped his black shirt on the ground for Lee Catherine to sit on. Soon, he was lying on top of her and then moving his hands inside her shirt, then inside her pants. Lee Catherine thought she probably should stop him, but it was hard to say no.

"Billy Joe. Billy Joe, wait a minute," and she put her hands on his to show him she meant it. "Don't. We shouldn't be doing this. I mean, it feels good and all, but we can't do this. It's just too much. My cousin Tilly said if a boy gets this far, you've got to stop or you might go all the way, and then you could get pregnant."

Billy Joe didn't argue with her. He just said, "Okay, why don't we go back and see if we can catch some more crawfish." They headed out of the woods, kneeled next to the big ditch and tied bacon fat on the end of their strings, which they'd tied to medium-sized sticks. Billy Joe hollered real loud when he caught one. But he threw it back. They always put the crawfish back so they'd be there next time. And anyway, these weren't the big crawfish that folks ate. They were just little ones that lived in the ditches by the fields and woods. There wouldn't be any point in killing them.

Traditional Recipes

Entrees

Red Beans and Rice Are Nice with Ham	43
Baked Chicken with Mushrooms in Foil	44
Second Line Jambalaya	45
Mama's Irish Stew	46
Lulu's Lost Chili	47
Carmen's Famous Gumbo	48
Mama's Beef Vegetable Soup	50

Side Dishes

Ferriday Fresh Fried Corn	51
Fancy Potato, Ham and Cheese Casserole	52
Mama's Mashed Potatoes	53
Mama's Macaroni and Cheese	54
Holiday Sweet Potato Casserole	55
Susie's Scratch Cornbread	56
Blair Street Waffle Cornbread	57
Southern Spicy Jalapeno Cornbread	58
Mama's Irish Potato Salad	59

Desserts

Sister Loves Chocolate Pie	60
Perfect Pumpkin Pie	61
Perfect Pecan Pie	62
Granny's Turtle Lake Spice Cookies	63
Show-Off Cheesecake	64

Recipe: RED BEANS AND RICE ARE NICE WITH HAM

Serves: 10

Ingredients

- ½ cup diced yellow onion
- 2 cloves minced garlic
- ½ cup chopped green onions
- 1 cup chopped celery
- ¼ cup chopped celery greens
- 1 cup of ¼-inch cubed smoked ham
- 3 cups dry red beans (kidney beans)
- 3 cups of water (to cook beans)
- ⅛ teaspoon sea salt
- ¼ teaspoon cayenne pepper
- ⅛ teaspoon ground black pepper
- ⅛ teaspoon red pepper flakes
- ⅛ teaspoon celery salt
- 1 teaspoon tamari (similar to soy sauce)
- 1 teaspoon hot sauce
- 2 cups cooked white rice

> SEE "HOW-TO SECTION" FOR INSTRUCTIONS ON PREPARING BEANS AND ON COOKING RICE. I SUGGEST YOU COOK THE RICE DURING THE LAST 40 MINUTES WHEN YOUR BEANS ARE COOKING.

Directions

Begin by chopping the onion, garlic, green onion, celery and celery greens, and ham. Put newly washed soaked beans into a pot or crockpot and add the vegetables, the spices, tamari and hot sauce. Fill the pot up to 1-inch from the top with approximately three cups of water and place on stove top. Heat on medium high and bring to a boil. Turn down slightly and let beans cook for 1 to 2 hours on medium high boil. Stir often, and watch the beans so that they do not run out of liquid or stick to the bottom of the pan. Add more water, if needed and "re-spice."

If using crockpot, set on high or low and let it cook away. Again, add water if it starts to dry out and "re-spice" if needed. Serve over white rice and if possible with Susie's Scratch Cornbread (recipe on page 56).

SUSIE'S NOTE

I will sometimes make twice as much of my spice mixture, add the first half and set the rest aside in case I need to "re-spice" later. In this way, I can make the flavor stronger without losing the balance of flavors involved. My mama always said, "Red Beans and Rice are nice, but remember to take your sweet time, since you must soak your beans! And be sure to make plenty for company!" By the way, I like a good Louisiana-style hot sauce. Crystal Hot Sauce is one of my favorites. I prefer more vinegar in the ones I use, but lots of folks love the hot, hot, hot ones!

Recipe: BAKED CHICKEN WITH MUSHROOMS IN FOIL

Serves: 6

Ingredients

- 2 ½ cups cooked rice
- 3 pounds of skinless chicken breast tenderloins
- 1 ¼ cups tamari (similar to soy sauce)
- 3 cups sliced mushrooms
- ½ cup medium chopped sweet yellow onion
- 2 cloves minced garlic
- ½ cup whole-wheat pastry flour
- 5 tablespoons ground ginger
- ½ teaspoon sea salt
- 1 teaspoon ground black pepper
- ¾ cup safflower oil
- 1 teaspoon toasted sesame oil
- 2 tablespoons butter
- ½ cup Chardonnay wine or broth
- 25 foot aluminum foil
- 1 cup sour cream
- ⅛ cup balsamic vinegar

SEE "HOW-TO SECTION" FOR HOW TO COOK RICE

Directions

Make rice and set aside. Rinse and pat chicken tenderloins and cut each in half, if large. Dry with paper towels. Cover breast pieces with tamari and place in a container in the refrigerator to marinate.

Slice mushrooms and set aside in bowl. Chop onions and garlic and set aside.

In a small glass bowl, combine the whole-wheat pastry flour and the powdered ginger with just a little bit of salt and black pepper. Mix the dry ingredients until ginger is well mixed into flour. Set aside.

Heat two 6- to 9-inch iron skillets over medium heat. In one skillet, place safflower oil and sesame oil. In the other, place butter. When butter melts and is getting hot, add garlic and mushrooms. Cover and cook for 5 minutes. Add Chardonnay or broth, stir gently, and let mixture come to a bubbly boil. Reduce heat to medium low and cook covered, stirring occasionally, for 10 to 15 minutes or until liquid is reduced almost completely.

Take breast pieces out of the fridge and remove from marinade. Pat them dry again, and then drop into the flour and ginger mixture. Coat well. Carefully place them one at a time in the skillet with safflower and sesame oil. Brown for 5 minutes. Turn each piece of chicken carefully with long cooking fork. Let brown another 5 minutes on the other side. Remove pieces and set on paper towels to drain.

Preheat oven to 350 degrees. Make 6 sets of foil pieces by taking 12-by-12-inch pieces of foil and folding them into triangles, once and then once again. Place a breast piece in the center of a piece of foil. Place ½ cup of rice on top of breast pieces. Place 1 tablespoon of chopped raw onions on rice. Place ¼ cup of mushrooms on top of that. Place 3 tablespoons of sour cream on top of that. Bring edges of foil together, gathering in the middle. It will look like a silver onion when done! Repeat process.

Place 6 chicken-in-foil packets on a cookie sheet and put in oven to cook for 30-35 minutes. Remove from oven and serve in foil. Drizzle with ¼ cup of tamari and ⅛ cup of balsamic vinegar mixed together.

SUSIE'S NOTE

This meal is a composite of flavors cooked on the stovetop then placed into the oven to finish cooking. Mama used to make this once we settled in on Elm Street in Fayetteville in Northwest Arkansas. I am not sure how she concocted it, but I loved it, as it reminds me of stroganoff due to the mushrooms. It's fine to use just about any mushroom that sautés up well and any kind of rice. I like brown basmati rice, as it adds a nutty flavor. I do want to share a tip. Make sure the heat in your skillet is medium to medium high to get a nice crisp on the chicken. This tastes great served with Ferriday Fresh-fried Corn.

Recipe: SECOND LINE JAMBALAYA

Serves: 10

Ingredients

- 2 large sweet yellow onions
- 9 cloves garlic
- 3 large red bell peppers
- 1 pound Andouille sausage
- 1 ½ pounds skinned and de-boned chicken breasts
- ¼ cup olive oil
- 1 teaspoon celery salt
- ½ teaspoon red pepper flakes
- ½ teaspoon sea salt
- ½ teaspoon ground black pepper
- 2 whole bay leaves
- 3 cups uncooked medium grain white rice
- 3 cups water
- 3 cups low-sodium chicken broth
- 1 cup green onions
- 3 tablespoons hot sauce

> SEE "HOW-TO SECTION" FOR INSTRUCTIONS ON ROASTING RED PEPPERS.

Directions

Chop onions into ½-inch pieces and set aside. Mince garlic along with roasted garlic from the peppers and set aside. Cut roasted red peppers into ½-inch pieces and set aside. Cut sausage into ½-inch cubes and place in a bowl. Cut chicken into 1-inch pieces.

Heat olive oil in a 9-inch cast iron skillet over medium heat. When skillet is very hot, add onions and garlic, sausage, and chicken.

Into a small bowl, place celery salt, red pepper flakes, sea salt and ground black pepper. Mix well. Sprinkle half of the spice mixture you have just created into the skillet. Saute in skillet for 10 to 15 minutes, stirring often.

Add roasted red pepper, uncooked rice, water, broth, the rest of the spices and bay leaf. Stir well. Bring to a boil. Cover and reduce heat for 30 to 45 minutes or until rice is tender and liquid has been completely absorbed. Take off stove and let rest in skillet for 5 to 10 minutes before serving.

Cut green onions into ¼-inch pieces. Use to garnish. Drizzle hot sauce on when serving.

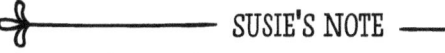

SUSIE'S NOTE

I always made this jambalaya after the Krewe of Drewe Parade in New Orleans. The Krewe of Drewe has a very local, working-class flavor. At this event, we would parade down the streets of Gentilly doing the Second Line. The Second Line is the second half of a jazz funeral. In a jazz funeral, the casket is led down the streets with mourners close behind and a marching jazz band playing a funeral dirge. At some point, the jazz band breaks into the jubilant notes of the Second Line and the mourners walk three steps forward and two steps back with joyful music meant to celebrate the deceased's life.

Recipe: MAMA'S IRISH STEW

Serves: 10

Ingredients

- 3 cups white or Yukon Gold potatoes, diced
- 2 cups carrots, chopped
- 2 cups celery, chopped
- 1 cup yellow onion, diced
- 1 clove garlic
- 2 cups beef stew meat, cubed
- 2 ¼ teaspoons sea salt
- 2 teaspoons ground black pepper
- ½ cup all purpose white flour
- 2 tablespoons canola oil
- ½ teaspoon tamari (similar to soy sauce)
- ¼ teaspoon powdered thyme
- ¼ teaspoon celery salt
- 1 whole bay leaf
- 4 cups water
- 2 cups cooked white rice

> SEE "HOW-TO SECTION" TO MAKE BROWN RICE. I SUGGEST YOU PREPARE THE RICE DURING THE LAST 40 MINUTES YOU ARE COOKING.

Directions

Cut up the potatoes, carrots, celery and onions into ½-inch pieces. Mince garlic fine. Also, cut beef into ½-inch cubes. Mix ¼ teaspoon sea salt and ¼ teaspoon ground pepper into 1 cup of flour. Take cut up beef and roll it in flour mixture to coat.

Heat 1 tablespoon of canola oil in a cast iron skillet on medium heat. Add the beef piece by piece to the skillet. Brown the beef for 10 minutes.

Add onions and garlic, the rest of the sea salt, the rest of the ground black pepper, tamari, thyme, celery salt and bay leaf. Add ½ cup of the water. Let simmer for 5 minutes.

Add potatoes, carrots, celery and the rest of the water. Stir gently with a wooden spoon. Let simmer on medium heat for 45 minutes or until all of the vegetables are thoroughly cooked and the broth is reduced to gravy. Add a little flour if thickening is needed.

Reduce to warm to serve. Remove the bay leaf. Serve over white rice. This is great with Susie's Scratch Cornbread (recipe on page 56).

— SUSIE'S NOTE —

I know Mama had to have learned this recipe from her mother-in-law, my Granny at Turtle Lake. It was our comfort food, and we made it to soothe us anytime it was cold and stormy outside.

Recipe: LULU'S LOST CHILI

Serves: 10

Ingredients

- 3 large red bell peppers
- 6 cloves garlic to be roasted with peppers
- 2 tablespoons ground cumin
- ¼ teaspoon celery salt
- ¼ teaspoon red pepper flakes
- ¼ teaspoon chili powder
- ¼ teaspoon cayenne pepper
- ½ teaspoon ground black pepper
- ½ teaspoon salt
- 1 cup celery, cut in ½-inch slices
- ¾ cup chopped yellow onion
- 2 ½ pounds lean ground round beef hamburger
- 2 tablespoons olive oil
- 16 ounces canned tomato sauce
- 6 ounces tomato paste
- 32 ounces canned whole tomatoes

SEE "HOW-TO SECTION" FOR INSTRUCTIONS ON PREPARING BEANS AND ROASTING PEPPERS AND GARLIC. PREPARE BOTH IN ADVANCE.

Directions

In a small bowl, combine cumin, celery salt, red pepper flakes, chili powder, cayenne pepper, ground black pepper and salt.

Cut the celery, onions, garlic, roasted garlic and roasted red pepper into ½-inch pieces, place into separate bowls and set aside.

Crumble the hamburger into a large bowl. Brown the meat uncovered in a 9-inch iron skillet over medium heat for approximately 15 minutes or until completely browned with a little of the spice mixture sprinkled on top. Remove the skillet and strain the liquid from the meat and set meat aside. Discard the liquid.

Heat skillet again on medium heat and add the olive oil. When the skillet is hot, add the celery, onions and garlic. Let the vegetables "sweat" by covering the skillet and cooking over medium heat for 10 minutes.

In a large stockpot, combine tomato sauce, browned meat, sweated vegetables, roasted red peppers, garlic, roasted garlic, the rest of the spices and tomato paste. Add the juice from the canned whole tomatoes. Cut up the whole tomatoes into small pieces and add to pot. Bring pot to boil then reduce to medium heat. Cook over medium to low heat covered, stirring often for 2 hours or until rich, thick and combined. Serve with Susie's Scratch Cornbread (recipe on page 56), saltine crackers or corn chips!

SUSIE'S NOTE

This was a recipe that my Aunt Lulu shared with my mother when I was about thirteen years old. Chili was kind of exotic in our house. The recipe Lulu developed was from her time in Peru while my uncle was working there in the 1960s. We often used the peppers Daddy would grow in Granny at Turtle Lake's garden.

Recipe: CARMEN'S FAMOUS GUMBO

Serves: 20

Ingredients

- 5- to 6-pound chicken, or two smaller chickens to equal 5 or 6 pounds
- 8 to 10 cups water
- 2 cups yellow onion chopped
- ½ whole yellow onion (not chopped)
- 1 sprig of rosemary
- 32 ounces canned whole tomatoes
- 5 tablespoons gumbo filé
- 1 teaspoon ground cayenne pepper
- 1 teaspoon celery salt
- 2 teaspoons salt
- 1 teaspoon fresh-ground black pepper
- 2 cups celery, chopped
- 3 cups okra, chopped
- 9 cloves garlic
- 1 cup green onions, sliced
- 3 large red bell peppers
- 16 ounces andouille sausage
- 2 tablespoons olive oil
- 1 ½ pounds fresh crabmeat
- ½ cup special draft beer
- ¼ cup all purpose flour (for roux)
- 3 tablespoons butter (for roux)

➤ This recipe takes 2 days.

Before you begin, please read about how to roast red peppers with garlic cloves and cook rice as described in the How-to Section, along with how to make roux.

Mix all dry spices together before preparing this dish. Rice should be made 40 minutes before gumbo is ready.

Directions

Day 1: After removing the bagged giblets from the chicken's cavity and discarding them, place whole chicken in large soup pot with water up to 1-inch from top of the pot. Add half of a whole yellow onion and a sprig of rosemary. Bring this to a boil and let it simmer for 2 hours.

Let cool down on stove for 2 hours. Refrigerate the pot with the chicken and broth overnight.

Day 2: Scoop the chicken fat off the top with a ladle. Discard (unless you have another use for it). Remove chicken from broth, and place it in a large bowl to debone and remove skin. Discard the bones and skin.

Place chicken in a medium-size bowl, and tear chicken into small pieces. Seal in container and refrigerate.

Strain chicken broth into a large stockpot to remove the onion and the rosemary. This chicken stock is your base for the gumbo.

Place the stockpot on the stove over medium heat. Cut up the canned tomatoes into small pieces and add them as well as their juices.

In a small bowl combine gumbo filé, cayenne pepper, celery salt, salt, and ground black pepper.

Cut into ½-inch pieces and place into separate bowls the remaining yellow onions, celery along with a bit of the greens, okra, the remaining garlic including the roasted garlic, green onions, roasted red peppers and sausage.

Place olive oil in a skillet over medium heat, and when hot, add onion, then garlic, then celery, as well as some of the cut-up celery leaves cut. Throw in just a little of the spice mixture. Let the onions, garlic and celery sauté for 7 minutes, stirring often.

Add ingredients from skillet into stockpot. Add the sausage, chicken, okra and roasted red peppers to the stockpot. Take the crab and pull it apart into small pieces. Add the crab to the stockpot. Add the remaining portion of the spice mixture. Add your favorite special draft beer, and then add roux. I usually put in a couple of teaspoons of it and then let the pot cook an hour. Then I check thickness and add more roux if it's not thick enough.

Cook on low to medium for a full day or more. Add Louisiana hot sauce to taste. Add more broth if gumbo seems too thick. Garnish with green onions. Serve over rice.

SUSIE'S NOTE

Gumbo is the proudest single thing a New Orleans resident can make. So much so, that on any given Saturday or Sunday in a local New Orleans neighborhood, say Gentilly or the Faubourg Marigny, you might find a friendly Gumbo Cook-off Showdown between neighbors sharing balconies or courtyards, the fragrance wafting ever so gently to their other neighbors, resulting in an impromptu Sunday night gathering with music, friends and the resulting gumbo treat!

When I was living there, we had gumbo cook-offs most weekends. We all had our secret ingredients. Mine was Sapporo Beer. I guess any special draft beer will do, but I am partial to Sapporo because it reminds me of a friend in New Orleans who would bring the frosty brown bottles home from work on hot summer days. We would place them in the freezer and take them out to enjoy when they were covered with ice.

Recipe: MAMA'S BEEF VEGETABLE SOUP

Serves: 8 to 10

Ingredients

- 1 teaspoon canola oil
- 1 cup all-purpose flour
- 1 teaspoon sea salt
- 1 teaspoon ground black pepper
- 2 cups beef soup meat
- 32 ounces canned whole tomatoes
- 3 cups potatoes, ½-inch dice
- 2 cups carrots, ½-inch dice
- 1 ½ cups celery, ½-inch slice
- 1 ½ cups yellow onion, ½-inch dice
- 1 cup green onions, ½-inch slice
- 3 cloves garlic
- 2 cups vegetable broth
- 2 cups water
- 8 ounces canned corn
- ¼ teaspoon cayenne pepper
- 1 tablespoon tamari (similar to soy sauce)
- 2 teaspoons Crystal hot sauce
- 1 teaspoon celery salt

Directions

In a small mixing bowl, combine the flour and a little bit of the salt and pepper and mix well.

Heat a 9-inch skillet to medium heat on stovetop with a teaspoon of canola oil. Dry off meat with paper towel and coat it, piece by piece, in the flour and salt and pepper. Add each piece of flour-coated meat to skillet. Brown the soup meat on both sides for eight minutes, and then take skillet off heat.

In a large stockpot (or crockpot), place the soup meat and the drippings from skillet. Now, add canned tomatoes, cut into little pieces, into the pot along with all the tomato juices from the can. Cut up the potatoes, celery, carrots, green onions and onions into ½-inch pieces. Add all of these vegetables to the stockpot. Mince the garlic and add to the pot. Add the vegetable broth, the water, the canned corn, the cayenne pepper, the tamari, the Crystal hot sauce and the celery salt.

If in a crockpot, set on high or low, depending on your schedule. On the stove, bring to a boil, cover and reduce to medium heat, and monitor as the soup cooks into goodness by an hour or so. This soup is best enjoyed with Southern Spicy Jalapeno Cornbread (recipe on page 58).

SUSIE'S NOTE

We would have starved to death if it were not for my Granny at Turtle Lake's garden. We ate soups and stews and savory meals all through my youth. As the years went by, someone in our immediate family always had a great garden!

✴ End of Entrees ✴

Recipe: FERRIDAY FRESH FRIED CORN

Serves: 8 to 10

Ingredients

- 15 ears white or yellow corn on the cob
- 8 ounces butter
- ½ teaspoon salt
- ¼ teaspoon black pepper
- 1 cup half-and-half
- ⅛ cup whole-wheat pastry flour

Directions

To cut and dress the corn, follow these instructions: Buy corn on the cob and pull off the husks and then pull off the silks in the sink. Run water over each corn on cob and get at any remaining silks. Do not leave silks on the cob, as they will end up in the skillet too!

Take a corn cob, cut off the knobby end, place the cob on a cutting board, flat cut end down, and run a thin sharp blade down the middle of each row of kernels. Turn the cob and repeat this process on each row of kernels, making sure to conserve any juice. After slicing the kernels this way, turn the knife flat and slice all of the kernels off the corn cob all the way down. This should take about 4 or 5 slices. Set aside with the corn and the juices and repeat with next cob.

Once you have finished with all the cobs, put a 9-inch skillet on medium heat and add the butter. When the butter gets so hot it is just about to burn, add the corn. Add the salt and pepper, and cover the corn and reduce the heat slightly. Let cook for 5 minutes stirring frequently but returning the lid to the pan to get a steaming effect.

After 5 minutes add the half-and-half slowly while stirring. Add only as much as needed to keep the mixture going and looking creamy. Cover and watch heat in skillet and keep just below boil.

In a small bowl, mix the whole-wheat pastry flour with salt and pepper. Open the skillet, and add a little of the flour slowly into the liquid. Stir. You only want to use a little of the flour, enough to make the corn thicken up a bit. Cook 5 minutes more, adding any additional half-and-half, if needed. Ferriday Fresh Fried Corn should be creamy, not sticky, not runny. The trick is in that detail!

SUSIE'S NOTE

This side dish was the kind of thing that I would wake up from a nap smelling as Mama would create a half dozen things for dinner in the evening.

Recipe: FANCY POTATO, HAM AND CHEESE CASSEROLE

Serves: 10

Ingredients

- 3 cups white or Yukon Gold potatoes
- 1 cup yellow onion, diced
- 1 cup ham, diced
- 1 ½ cups sharp cheddar cheese, 1 cup diced and ½ cut shredded
- 1 teaspoon olive oil
- 2 cups whole milk
- ½ teaspoon salt
- ¾ teaspoon fresh ground pepper

Directions

Wash and peel the potatoes. Slice the potatoes into fairly uniform thin scalloped slices. Cut the potato slices in half as well. Set aside in a glass bowl and cover with water.

Dice the onion into ½-inch chunks and place into small bowl and set aside.

Dice the ham into ¼-inch chunks; set aside.

Cut 1 cup of the cheese into quarter inch chunks and set aside. Grate the rest of the cheese and set aside.

Heat oven to 325 degrees.

Use a long rectangular oven-safe casserole dish, and oil the bottom of the dish by hand with olive oil.

Re-rinse and drain the potatoes. Shake out as much water as you can. Place a layer of potatoes on the bottom of the casserole dish. Add a layer of onion, ham and cheese.

Add another layer of potatoes, and then add another layer of onions, ham and cheese. Continue until up to the top or you are out of ingredients.

Add milk, salt and pepper. Mix the milk and salt and pepper into the layers a bit without messing them up too much. Top the whole thing with half a cup grated cheese.

Pop into oven for 35 to 45 minutes. Test if done by sticking fork into the potatoes. The potatoes should be soft. Take out and let cool for 5 minutes before serving. Ladle out with a spoon. Great with Baked Chicken with Ginger in Foil.

SUSIE'S NOTE

This stand-by was a great nutritional money saver in our house growing up. It was a way to get protein and veggies and starch and end up with a delicious meal. The kids always love this--kind of a scalloped potato dish but with ham. It's always a crowd pleaser. I make this for the family nearly every holiday and at home for me when I need a little comfort.

Recipe: MAMA'S MASHED POTATOES

Serves: 10

Ingredients

- 4 cups red or Yukon Gold potatoes, diced
- 6 cups water
- 1 teaspoon salt
- 4 ounces unsalted sweet cream butter
- 1 teaspoon fresh ground pepper
- ½ cup whole milk

Directions

Wash and peel potatoes. Cut potatoes into 2-inch chunks. Have a big glass bowl partially filled with water to drop potatoes into when cut up as process progresses. This way, potatoes do not turn brown.

After all potatoes are cut up, prepare a large stockpot by partially filling it with water. Drain the potatoes and add them gently to the new water in the stockpot. Add a little of the salt to the water in the pot. Make sure the pot has water covering all of the potatoes. Also watch to make sure the pot is not too full, as you do not want it to boil over while cooking.

Place the stockpot with potatoes and water on the stove on high heat. Bring to a boil, then reduce heat to medium and cover the stockpot. Continue to boil stockpot, stirring occasionally. Boil potatoes until tender. Test by removing a potato and sticking a fork into it. If the fork goes through very easily, they are done. If there is any resistance, potatoes are not done. This should take about 45 minutes.

When done, remove stockpot with potatoes from the stove and drain them into a colander to remove the water. Place the drained potatoes into a large glass mixing bowl. Cut the butter stick into four pieces. Add butter to the potatoes, let melt partially. Add the rest of the salt and the pepper and a little bit of the milk. Now, you can either mix potatoes by hand with a fork or strong whisk or do so with a hand mixer or counter mixer. Add more milk as you go. The end result should be fairly smooth and creamy.

SUSIE'S NOTE

Mama's Mashed Potatoes, while simple-sounding as a dish, can be hard for some to pull off. I decided to include it here because it was one of my favorite dishes growing up, and I still love making it anytime I am with family. If it's a holiday, sure enough one of us will whip up some 'taters. Sometimes, a sibling will get brave and add a clove or two of roasted garlic into it as well, just to see if anybody will notice!

Recipe: MAMA'S MACARONI AND CHEESE

Serves: 8 to 10

Ingredients

- 2 cups sharp cheddar cheese, diced
- 4 cups water
- ¼ teaspoon olive oil
- 7 ounces thin vermicelli-style pasta
- 2 tablespoons sweet cream butter
- 2 cups whole milk
- ¼ teaspoon salt
- ¼ teaspoon ground black pepper

Directions

Preheat oven to 350 degrees.

Cut cheese into half-inch chunks and set aside.

Place water in a stockpot to boil. Drop olive oil into the water once it comes to a boil and add the vermicelli. Reduce the heat and stir the vermicelli so that is separates as much as possible. Boil for 5 minutes or until done. The pasta is done when a few pieces of vermicelli can be wrapped around a fork and are tender yet just getting slippery, not overdone. This is al dente. When done, strain the vermicelli and set aside.

Place hot strained vermicelli into a large casserole dish. Add butter to vermicelli by cutting butter into small pieces and placing it between the folds of the vermicelli. Allow it to melt for three minutes. When the butter is melted, toss the vermicelli with the butter in the casserole until vermicelli is well coated. Add chunks of cheese. Place the cheese in between the folds of the vermicelli, under it evenly, and then more on top. Add the milk to the dish. Season with salt and pepper.

Place the casserole in 350 degree oven and bake for 30 minutes uncovered. Remove from oven and let cool 5 minutes before serving. Cut into squares while in the dish. Wonderful served as a side dish accompanying Red Beans and Rice Are Nice with Ham (recipe on page 43).

— SUSIE'S NOTE —

I loved this dish from my Mama. I am not sure if she came up with this, but it must have been her own invention. We kids all liked the "skinny" spaghetti, and she found a way to put it into a dish that was quick and easy for her or one of us girls to make anytime.

Recipe: HOLIDAY SWEET POTATO CASSEROLE

Serves: 10

Ingredients

- 1 tablespoon sweet cream butter
- 3 cups sweet potatoes
- ½ teaspoon nutmeg
- ⅛ teaspoon salt
- ½ teaspoon cinnamon
- ¼ cup brown sugar
- 1 cup water

Directions

Grease a large rectangular glass oven-safe baking pan with 1 tablespoon of butter. Heat oven to 350 degrees.

Either peel the sweet potatoes or leave the skins on, and slice them into scallop style. The slices should be uniform and about ⅛-inch thick. Place the sliced sweet potatoes into the casserole dish splayed out like a deck of cards in rows. Do so until all slices are used up and entire casserole is full.

In a small dish or bowl, mix the nutmeg, salt and cinnamon. Sprinkle the mixture over the top of the entire casserole. Crumble the brown sugar over the casserole as evenly as possible. Add enough water to come to ½-inch from the top of the dish.

Place the dish into the 350 degree oven for 40 minutes or until sweet potatoes are tender. Check the dish occasionally while cooking, and add additional water if the dish becomes dry. It should still have a bit of moisture at the end of cooking time. Remove from oven when done and let cool for at least 5 minutes before serving. Great with holiday dinners like turkey and dressing.

SUSIE'S NOTE

Sweet potatoes and yams were fairly interchangeable. All I know is one way or another we used them to make this dish. I think we had nothing but sweet potatoes, but we called them yams. Only when I came out to California did I notice the difference. High in mineral content and rich and tasty—you can almost eat them with nothing added at all, but I love to cook them up like my Mama did.

Recipe: SUSIE'S SCRATCH CORNBREAD

Serves: 8 to 10

Ingredients

- 3 tablespoons corn oil
- 2 cups finely ground cornmeal
- 1 cup whole-wheat pastry flour
- 4 teaspoons baking powder
- ¼ teaspoon salt
- 2 large eggs
- 1 ½ cups old fashioned buttermilk (churned buttermilk rather than cultured)

Directions

Begin by heating your oven to 425 degrees. When oven is heated pour 2 tablespoons of corn oil into a 9-inch cast iron skillet, and place the skillet into the hot oven.

Place a sifter of some kind over a large bowl. Measure out the cornmeal into the sifter, then add the whole-wheat pastry flour, the baking powder and salt. Sift all ingredients into the big bowl. Make sure all of these dry ingredients are well mixed.

Remove the sifter device and add the eggs and half of the old-fashioned buttermilk. Begin mixing this together with a hand whisk. Add more of the buttermilk as needed to make a batter the consistency of cake batter. Add the remaining tablespoon of corn oil.

Carefully remove the skillet from the oven. Pour half of the hot corn oil from the skillet into the batter. Mix into batter lightly with fork. Pour batter into skillet and put into hot oven for 45 minutes or until top of cornbread is golden brown.

Remove from oven and turn cornbread out onto a plate. Bottom side should be up and should be showing. Then let cornbread sit for 5 minutes, and slice like a pie and serve. Split the "pie pieces" lengthwise and slip butter inside.

--- SUSIE'S NOTE ---

I learned to make this cornbread when I was nine years old. Anytime our family had cornbread at a meal, it was my duty to make it. As cornbread was one of our staples, this happened about five times a week, so I learned to make really good cornbread!

Traditional Recipes: Side Dishes

Recipe: BLAIR STREET WAFFLE CORNBREAD
Serves: 5 waffles

Ingredients

- Pam spray
- ½ cup cheddar cheese, ⅛-inch chunks
- ¼ cup finely chopped onion
- ½ cup drained canned corn
- 1 tablespoon minced jalapeno
- 2 large eggs
- ½ teaspoon salt
- ½ cup vegetable oil
- 1 cup cormeal
- 1 cup while wheat pastry flour
- 1 cup buttermilk or soy creamer
- 1 ½ tablespoon baking powder
- 1 teaspoon jalapeno juice

Directions

Begin by cutting up the cheese and setting it aside in a small bowl. Next, chop the onions fine and set aside in a small bowl. Then open the canned corn, drain and set aside. Mince the jalapenos and also set them aside. Next, beat the eggs until they are foamy. Add in the oil and buttermilk or soy creamer. Sift your cornmeal, flour, salt, and baking powder into the eggs while whisking. Add the cheese to the batter and stir it in with a wooden spoon. Add in the onions and the jalapenos, then add in the corn and the jalapeno juice. Stir well with the wooden spoon.

Use a soup ladle to ladle the batter into the waffle iron covering only half of the bottom griddle. Close and cook on medium high setting until golden brown. Repeat process to make more waffle bread. Serve topped with salsa or green tomato relish.

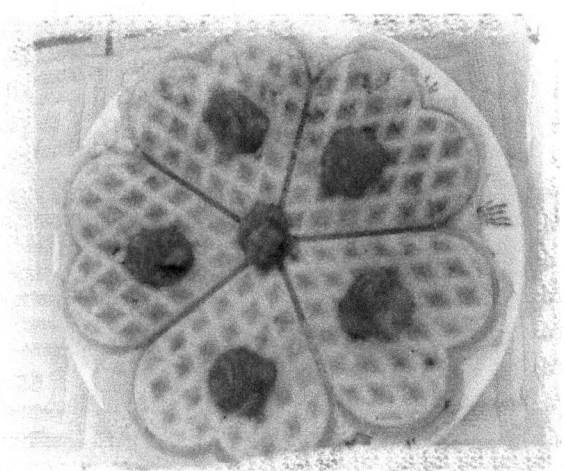

SUSIE'S NOTE

This is a recipe I developed with my buddy Richard Sherin. We used to make a version of this for all of the friends, the kids and anyone else passing by. They would all be drawn to Blair Street to share their tales of adventure from last night and Richie's tasty treats. Sometimes, he would make waffle bread all day long! He often used Government Cheese but I think it comes out better with cheddar.

Recipe: SOUTHERN SPICY JALAPENO CORNBREAD

Serves: 8 to 10

Ingredients

- 8 ounces sharp cheddar cheese
- 8 ounces yellow onion
- 8 ounces canned corn
- 4 ounces jalapeno
- 3 tablespoons corn oil
- 2 cups finely ground cornmeal
- 1 cup whole wheat pastry flour
- ¼ teaspoon salt
- 4 teaspoons baking powder
- 2 large eggs
- 16 ounces old-fashioned buttermilk (churned buttermilk, not cultured)
- 2 ounces of juice from the jalapeno jar

Directions

It's best to cut up the onion and jalapeno in advance and set aside. Also best to have the cubed sharp cheddar cheese in a bowl, as well as the canned corn.

Begin by cutting up the cheese into ½-inch chunks, and place into a small bowl and set aside. Cut up the onion into ½-inch pieces, and set aside in another small bowl. Open the corn and drain off the water and set aside. Cut jalapeno slices into minced pieces and set aside.

Heat your oven to 425 degrees and put 2 tablespoons of the corn oil into a 9-inch cast iron skillet. Put skillet into hot oven for at least 10 minutes--in that amount of time you can assemble the cornbread batter.

Sift together the cornmeal and the whole-wheat pastry flour, as well as the salt and the baking powder, into a large bowl. Add 2 eggs and about half of the buttermilk, and mix the batter together with a whisk. Add the rest of the buttermilk to form a fairly thick batter. Add the other 1 tablespoon of corn oil, and stir in lightly. If the mixture seems too dry, add a bit more buttermilk. The mixture should be a little bit thicker than a cake batter.

Add the drained corn, the onion, the jalapeno and the cheese. Fold these into the batter with a spoon. Add the 2 ounces of jalapeno juice from the jalapeno jar. Mix lightly.

With a good oven mitt, take the skillet out of the oven and pour some of the excess oil in the skillet into the batter. Place the skillet back on the stovetop. Mix the oil in lightly with a fork. Pour the jalapeno cornbread batter into the skillet, then place the skillet back into oven.

Bake for 40 minutes or until knife into center of cornbread comes out clean. Remove cornbread from oven, and turn over onto a plate. Cut into pie-like pieces and enjoy with a meal!

SUSIE'S NOTE

This dish is one of my absolute favorite things. I make it at least once a week. You can re-heat the cornbread pieces and eat it all week by cutting the cornbread into pie-shaped pieces and then slicing the pie piece lengthwise. Place the pieces under the broiler or in toaster oven to toast. Once nice and crispy brown, top with butter or your favorite salsa and enjoy!

Recipe: MAMA'S IRISH POTATO SALAD

Serves: 10

Ingredients

- 3 cups small red or Yukon Gold potatoes
- 5 cups water
- ½ teaspoon salt
- 1 cup sweet Vidalia onions, chopped
- ½ cup green onions, sliced
- 1 cup celery and celery greens, chopped
- 1 cup red bell peppers, chopped
- 1 ½ cups cherry tomatoes
- ¼ teaspoon celery salt
- ½ teaspoon fresh-ground black pepper
- 1 cup mayonnaise
- 2 tablespoons brown mustard
- 1 cup sour cream
- 1 cup yogurt
- ⅛ cup Balsamic vinegar

Directions

Rinse small red or Yukon Gold potatoes in colander under cold running water. Remove any eyes and dirt. Cut the potatoes into 1-inch chunks while leaving the skin on the potatoes. Place the potatoes into a large stockpot and cover them with cool water to 1-inch from the top, and add a little bit of the salt. Put the stockpot on medium to high heat on the stove until it comes to a boil, then turn down slightly and boil potatoes for 45 minutes or until fork goes into potato easily.

While the potatoes are cooking, cut the onions, the green onions, the celery and the red bell peppers into ¼-inch pieces. Be sure to remove the seeds and ribs of the bell pepper when preparing it to be cut up. Set the cut vegetables in a large bowl together and set aside.

Remove the stockpot from the heat and drain the potatoes into a colander in sink. Let the potatoes cool for 30 minutes. Place the cooled potatoes into a large glass bowl and add the onions, green onions, celery, red bell pepper and cherry tomatoes. Add the salt, celery salt and black pepper. Then add the mayonnaise, mustard, sour cream, yogurt and vinegar. Stir slowly and carefully with a wooden spoon. Fold everything together, taking care not to break the tomatoes. Refrigerate for 6 hours, then serve.

— SUSIE'S NOTE —

At Christmas, our family chooses one central location, and then we all make tasty dishes and bring them over potluck style. It's been this way ever since my Mama died, and I think it let's all of us participate and share and takes the pressure off of the sibling hosting the party. A few years ago, my sister Amy and I decided to make some good old-fashioned potato salad. I added cherry tomatoes for an interesting twist.

* End of Side Dishes *

Recipe: SISTER LOVES CHOCOLATE PIE

Serves: 8 to 10

Ingredients

- 1 9-inch baked pastry pie crust
- 1/3 cup all-purpose flour
- 1 cup sugar
- ¼ teaspoon salt
- 2 (1 ounce) squares unsweetened baking chocolate
- 2 cups whole milk
- 3 beaten egg yolks
- 2 tablespoons sweet cream butter
- ½ teaspoon vanilla extract
- 3 egg whites
- 6 tablespoons sugar

Directions:

This is Mama's recipe as made by my sister Amy.

In a large glass bowl, mix the flour, sugar and salt. Melt the chocolate in milk in a double boiler, heating until the milk is scalded. Gradually add the flour, sugar and salt mixture and cook over moderate heat. Stir constantly until the mixture thickens and boils. Cook for another 2 minutes.

Remove from heat, and add a small amount of this hot mixture to the egg yolks and stir. Then add the egg yolks to the chocolate mixture. Cook for 1 minute, stirring constantly.

Turn off the heat! Add butter and vanilla, and stir. Let it cool a bit. Pour it into the baked pie shell, and let it cool some more.

Now it's time to make the meringue. This is easy. Just beat the egg whites stiff while gradually adding the sugar. You may want to trim the sugar down from six tablespoons to 4 or 5 instead, if you like the meringue less sweet and more fluffy. Cover the top of the pie with the meringue to make sure it seals around all the edges of the pie plate Bake at 350 degrees for 15 minutes or until the meringue is browned.

AMY'S NOTE

I remember Mama going to work at the bank in the summertime, and I'd be at home with my brothers and my little sister. I was about nine. I'd be hungry for pie and itching to bake one myself and be all grown up. Mama would leave ready-to-bake homemade pie crust in the freezer in pie plates ready to go! I'd pull one out and start cooking the chocolate pudding on the gas stove. Oh, how I loved chocolate then, and I do love it now! Once, I forgot to put the egg yolks in the pudding part, and I went and fed some to our neighbor, Dennis. He said it was really good anyway. I never forgot that. He was kind when he could have been mean to me. He was older, and I was used to getting made fun of by the older boys. But not that day. God bless you Dennis!

Recipe: PERFECT PUMPKIN PIE

Serves: 8 to 10

Crust Ingredients

- 2 tablespoons raw granulated sugar
- 2 cups roasted almonds
- 1 cup powdered sugar
- 1/3 cup sweet cream butter, plus 1 tablespoon to grease the pie plate

Filling Ingredients

- 3/4 cup granulated white sugar
- 1 1/4 teaspoons ground cinnamon
- 1/2 teaspoon salt
- 1/4 teaspoon ground ginger
- 1/8 teaspoon ground nutmeg
- 15 ounces pumpkin puree
- 16 ounces Eagle Brand condensed milk
- 2 large eggs

SEE "HOW-TO SECTION" FOR INSTRUCTIONS ON ROASTING AND GRINDING ALMONDS.

Almonds should be roasted ahead of time and allowed to cool before grinding them to use in making the pie crust.

The crust must be made first and set aside to cool for at least 45 minutes prior to using it.

This pie is meant to be made a day in advance and refrigerated to serve the next day.

Directions for Crust:

Preheat oven to 350 degrees.

To prepare the crust, begin by greasing a pie plate with butter. Then pour 2 tablespoons of sugar into the greased pie plate and rotate the pan until it is completely coated with the sugar. Remove any excess sugar from the pie plate by turning it upside down over the sink.

In a medium glass bowl, combine finely ground roasted almonds and powdered sugar. Mix them together well. Add softened butter and form into a kind of dough. Add the mixture to the pie plate, forming the crust as you go. It should look and perform just like a graham cracker crust.

Bake the crust for 10 minutes at 350 degrees. Take crust out and let it cool for at least 45 minutes before adding the pie filling and baking the pie.

Directions for Filling:

Preheat oven to 425 degrees.

For the filling, take a large bowl. In it, mix sugar, cinnamon, salt, ginger and nutmeg. Add to this the pumpkin puree, condensed milk and eggs. After all the ingredients are in, whisk until well blended. Pour mixture into the baked almond piecrust.

Place the pie on the bottom rack of a 425-degree oven. Bake for 15 minutes, then reduce temperature to 350 degrees and continue baking for another 45 minutes or until a knife inserted into the middle of the pie comes out clean.

Set pie on a rack and let it cool for 2 hours. Refrigerate pie overnight and then serve.

SUSIE'S NOTE

I have served this more traditional version of Pumpkin Pie to family and friends from Louisiana to Arkansas to California for many years. It is my favorite part of the holiday meal, especially at Thanksgiving.

Recipe: PERFECT PECAN PIE
Serves: 8 to 10

Crust Ingredients
- 2 tablespoons raw granulated sugar
- 2 cups roasted almonds
- 1 cup powdered sugar
- 1/3 cup sweet cream butter, plus 1 tablespoon to grease the pie plate

Filling Ingredients
- 2 cups pecans, 1 ½ cup chopped, ½ cup whole
- 3 beaten eggs
- 1 ½ cups honey
- 1 ½ cups brown sugar
- 1 teaspoon vanilla extract
- 1/8 teaspoon salt

SEE "HOW-TO SECTION" FOR INSTRUCTIONS ON ROASTING AND GRINDING ALMONDS.

Almonds should be roasted ahead of time and allowed to cool before grinding them to use in making the pie crust.

The crust must be made first and set aside to cool for at least 45 minutes prior to using it.

Directions for Crust:
Preheat oven to 350 degrees.

To prepare the crust, begin by greasing a pie plate with butter. Then pour 2 tablespoons of sugar into the greased pie plate and rotate the pan until it is completely coated with the sugar. Remove any excess sugar from the pie plate by turning it upside down over the sink.

In a medium glass bowl, combine finely ground roasted almonds and powdered sugar. Mix them together well. Add softened butter and form into a kind of dough. Add the mixture to the pie plate, forming the crust as you go. It should look and perform just like a graham cracker crust.

Bake the crust for 10 minutes at 350 degrees. Take crust out and let it cool for at least 45 minutes before adding the pie filling and baking the pie.

Directions for Filling:
For this recipe it is best to have three glass bowls, a small one, a medium one and a large one. Place the bowls on the kitchen counter and proceed.

On a large cutting board, chop 1 ½ cups pecans to a medium chop. Add the chopped pecans to the medium bowl and set aside. Keep half a cup of the pecans whole and set aside from the rest.

In the small bowl, crack 3 eggs and beat well with a whisk. Set the eggs aside.

In the large bowl, combine honey, brown sugar, vanilla and salt, and stir with wooden spoon. Add the eggs to the large bowl one third at a time, stirring with the wooden spoon. Add the chopped pecans to the large bowl, and stir them in.

Turn out mixture into pre-made pie crust, either the homemade almond crust mentioned above or a store-bought crust. Place pie into preheated 350 degree oven and bake for 35 minutes. Remove from oven and place on a wire rack to cool. Cover and refrigerate when cooled. Enjoy!

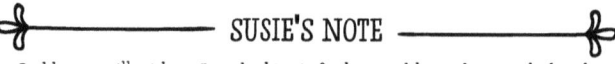

SUSIE'S NOTE

When my Daddy was still with us, I made this pie for him and he said it was the best he ever had. He was the original country boy chef, so coming from him this was a high honor!

Recipe: GRANNY'S TURTLE LAKE SPICE COOKIES
Makes: 15-20 cookies

Ingredients
- 1 cup sweet cream butter (softened)
- 4 beaten eggs
- 1 cup chopped pecans
- 2 cups brown sugar
- 2 teaspoons vanilla extract
- 1 teaspoon ground cinnamon
- ½ teaspoon ground cloves
- ½ teaspoon ground allspice
- 1 cup oatmeal
- 3 cups self-rising flour

Directions

For this recipe, your butter will need to be soft. Take the butter out of the refrigerator at least 1 hour before you plan to begin to make the cookies.

Cut pecans up very fine and set aside in a small bowl.

In a small bowl, beat the eggs into the softened butter until combined fully.

In a large bowl, combine brown sugar, vanilla extract, ground cinnamon, ground cloves, ground allspice, pecans and oatmeal. Stir in the butter and eggs mixture and combine thoroughly. Add the flour.

Then bake at 375 degrees for 10 minutes. Remove from oven and use a spatula to loosen each one from bottom of pan. Let cool or eat hot!

SUSIE'S NOTE

My Aunt Frankie says there was a secret ingredient Granny always put in. It seems it was whatever brown liquor Papaw kept under the counter, just a dash.

Recipe: SHOW-OFF CHEESECAKE
Serves: 8 to 10

This cheesecake is meant to be made a day in advance and refrigerated to serve the next day.

Crust Ingredients
- 2 tablespoons raw granulated sugar
- 2 cups roasted almonds
- 1 cup powdered sugar
- 1/3 cup sweet cream butter, plus 1 tablespoon to grease the pie plate

Filling Ingredients
- 3 large eggs
- 32 ounces cream cheese
- 16 ounces sour cream
- 1 cup granulated white sugar
- 1/2 teaspoon vanilla extract
- 16 ounce bar organic dark chocolate (optional)

> SEE "HOW-TO SECTION" FOR INSTRUCTIONS ON ROASTING AND GRINDING ALMONDS.
>
> Almonds should be roasted ahead of time and allowed to cool before grinding them to use in making the pie crust.
>
> The crust must be made first and set aside to cool for at least 45 minutes prior to using it.

Directions for Crust:
Preheat oven to 350 degrees.

To prepare the crust, begin by greasing a pie plate with butter. Then pour 2 tablespoons of sugar into the greased pie plate and rotate the pan until it is completely coated with the sugar. Remove any excess sugar from the pie plate by turning it upside down over the sink.

In a medium glass bowl, combine finely ground roasted almonds and powdered sugar. Mix them together well. Add softened butter and form into a kind of dough. Add the mixture to the pie plate, forming the crust as you go. It should look and perform just like a graham cracker crust.

Bake the crust for 10 minutes at 350 degrees. Take crust out and let it cool for at least 45 minutes before adding the pie filling and baking the pie.

Directions for Filling:
Preheat oven to 350 degrees.

This recipe works best with 1 large glass bowl and 2 small ones.

First, crack 3 large eggs into one of the small glass bowls. Beat eggs by hand or with hand mixer until they are beaten well. Set the beaten eggs aside.

Into large bowl, place the cream cheese, sour cream, sugar and vanilla. Mix with a hand mixer or with a whisk. Add eggs to mixture slowly 1/3 of the eggs at a time. If desired, to make it really "show-off," cut dark chocolate into 1/4-inch chunks, and stir into the cheesecake batter.

Turn out mixture from large glass bowl into pre-cooked almond pie crust. Place the cheesecake into oven at 350 degrees for 35 minutes. Remove from oven and cool on wire rack until almost room temperature.

Cover cheesecake and refrigerate overnight. Remove from fridge, cut into pie pieces and serve.

 SUSIE'S NOTE

I have made this cheesecake many times since I was a teenager. Nobody really taught me how to make it. I just figured it out. I added the dark chocolate once in New Orleans for Polly's son on his birthday. Ever since then I call it "Show-Off" Cheesecake. Need I say more? Make it, and your guests will drool!

Recipe Notes:

* End of Desserts *

Lizards, Spiders and Snakes
by Amylou Wilson

Mama didn't mean to do things that would make Daddy mad. But he got angry and frustrated with her all the time, and us children, too. Mostly, it had to do with not doing something just like he told you to do it.

Take the day Mama hacked the green snake to death in her rose garden. She didn't always know the difference between a good snake and a bad one. All she knew was that deadly snakes lived all around her, and she didn't want any snake to get her or one of her children. Rattlers were common around Ferriday, Louisiana, and cottonmouths, too, especially where there was any swampy water.

The morning Mama killed the snake started out with a bang, literally. The sound of the front screened door slamming and the salesman screeching as he turned and ran to his car to escape.

He'd knocked on the front door, and Mama was inside the kitchen baking pecan pies. It was Saturday, and Daddy had long since headed to his mother's farm down the road to sit on the back porch with his father, smelling the aroma wafting from the fig trees that ran along the side of the farmhouse. They drank thick dark roast Community Coffee.

Anyway, Mama wiped her hands on a dishtowel and headed for the door. She noticed the stranger's car from the living room windows as she made her way there. The screened door wasn't latched.

"Mornin', ma'am."

Louise opened the door. The man held a large, heavy case in one hand. She'd heard from Norma, her nearest neighbor across the gravel road and a stretch of woods, that a man had been in the neighborhood selling Electrolux vacuums door-to-door. Norma bought one, and she was eagerly waiting for it to be delivered. Mama was halfway interested in it. It was supposed to be a revolutionary new vacuum, but she'd have to see Norma's first. And then, if she really liked it, she'd have to save and convince my daddy she really needed it.

They didn't have much extra money in those days, she and John. But they had a good life. Mama didn't make many large purchases on her own, and she was very careful with money.

"Good morning," Mama said.

"Ma'am, thanks for taking a moment to ... ah ... what the ..." and the man screamed and began slapping at his head. Mama didn't know why he was hitting himself, but she'd come to the door armed with a broom just in case. She started to beat him with it and told him to "get out, get out of my house!"

Of course, Lee Catherine and her little sister, Mags, came running as fast as they could. When they got there, they saw several green lizards scattered about on the floor by the door. By that time, the salesman was in his car backing out of the driveway and peeling out fast onto the pea-gravel road, where sparks were flying in the sunlight.

"Mama, Mama look, look!" Lee Catherine yelled excitedly. "Look at all the lizards!"

Their mother began to laugh uncontrollably. "Goodness gracious alive," she exclaimed as she laughed. "That poor man ..."

Lee Catherine and Mags laughed too, and their mother, Louise, began sweeping the lizards across the wood floor and out the door onto the front porch, then down the steps to the grassy yard. A couple of lizards seemed stunned, but all were still alive. They all laughed some more and Louise's blue-green eyes were filled with tears.

This may sound strange to anyone who doesn't live here, but it was common for lizards to gather on the window screens and screened doors of the house depending on the time of year. Usually, there weren't a whole lot of lizards gathered on the front porch screen door, perhaps because the door on this side of the house sat highest from the ground. That means lizards might be there, but you didn't necessarily notice them. At the back door by the clothesline, on the other hand, lizards often could be found totally covering the surface.

"Why don't you two girls come help me finish up these pecan pies? I could use a hand mixing the pecans in before they go in the oven."

They followed her to the kitchen, which had a long black and white tiled bar on one side that overlooked the large den from an elevation of about six feet. Lee Catherine's father, John, had spent an entire year at home once in order to add on to the house. The den, laundry room and another bathroom were built from the ground up from a concrete slab base. The walls of the house contained a double layer of red bricks that her father laid himself, for he was a master brick mason. A large fireplace and mantle served as the focal point at one end of the den. The ceilings were very tall, and Lee Catherine felt she and her family lived spaciously. They even had a washer and a dryer, too. No more hanging out clothes, spending the day sorting dirty laundry, washing, hanging them out on the clothesline to dry, or worse, sitting for hours in the little laundromat in downtown Ferriday, reading and folding, reading and folding. Then returning home to press creases into Daddy's cement-crusted khakis. Lee Catherine could smell his sweat steaming out as she ironed, for it could never be completely washed away.

The addition to the house also included the double garage, which had been converted into "the boys' room." Each boy had his own bed and space there, but privacy had its limits. John gave Mama a little shuttered window in the kitchen above her sink. It opened up to the boys' room. Mama could peer down and see Little John, Patrick, and Jimmy anytime she wanted, but she was a good mother. Her children had a right to some privacy, just like she did. And she respected that.

Lee Catherine and Magdalene, her little sister who was known as Mags, sat on stools at the bar overlooking the big den and began stirring pecans into the gooey mixture. Mags measured out a half cup of pecan halves at a time and sprinkled them into the mixing bowl, while Lee Catherine stirred the pecans in by hand. Sometimes, Lee Catherine got some of the filling on her fingers, and when she did, she'd lick the sticky stuff off with abandon. It wasn't considered gross or disgusting to do this, at least not in her mama's kitchen. That was simply one of the perks of cooking and baking. And if someone didn't like it, then they didn't have to eat your food.

Louise busied herself washing dishes at the sink while she gazed down into the boys' room. She was thinking about more housework.

Tomorrow, she'd make the boys strip their beds and put new sheets on, then she'd have Jimbo dust and she would follow up with the vacuum. First, she would have to take the broom and a ladder and go at the spider webs she spied in the upper corners of the room.

Like it or not, spiders lived in the house with them, no matter how hard Louise tried to keep them out. At this very moment, a black widow was carefully spinning its web in a corner of the molding under the bar in the kitchen, right where Mags' knees jutted out on the stool. When Mags felt the creepy, crawly creature on her left thigh, she reared back on the stool, fell backwards, and Mags and pecans flew to the floor. As the stool and Mags went flying back, her head hit the formica kitchen table.

Mags was screaming and crying, as much about hitting her head as she was about the pecans scattered around her. She was only six years old, and she hated it when she disappointed her mother.

Mags finally calmed down enough to tell Lee Catherine and her mother what made her rear back like that, and the two of them began looking everywhere for the spider, if indeed there was one. Louise was known for keeping a tidy house, and spider webs and poisonous spiders were not welcome here. Lee Catherine got the broom and swished it under the bar. They found the web, but never caught sight of the black widow. Louise knew it would turn up eventually, though.

As they cleaned pecans off the floor and positioned Mags at the kitchen table to finish helping with the pies, a granddaddy longlegs was making his way across the green shag carpet in the den, lumbering toward the old upright piano against the wall. Granddaddies were okay because they couldn't hurt you and were fun to watch. Also, they were easy to exit from the house. Softly pinch one of a granddaddy's many legs between two fingers and toss it out the door. There was a kind of unwritten law in this part of the country, one about not killing creatures that meant you no harm. It was taken very seriously by most folks.

Louise put the pecan pies in the oven to bake and the girls took turns scraping with spoons and eating every bit of stuff left in the mixing bowl. Then, Lee Catherine offered to finish the dishes. She wasn't tall enough yet to reach the sink, so she pulled up a kitchen chair to reach everything. Mags watched, secretly glad that she was still too young and small to wash dishes. She wanted her sister to hurry up and finish so they could go outside and play. Louise decided now would be a good time to vacuum the den, while the boys and John weren't home.

"Why don't y'all go out and play while I finish some housework?" she offered to Lee Catherine and Mags. "Then, we'll work some in the flowerbeds."

Mags and Lee Catherine raced each other outside, exiting through the back door located at the laundry room off the den. The possibilities for play seemed endless. They could ride their bicycles up and down the gravel road and practice spinning out on the pea gravel, or play tetherball, or shoot baskets on the homemade basketball court. The basketball court shared space with two huge barbecue pits. Their daddy had poured a concrete slab under the goal to make it easy to retrieve the ball and play games like "horse." But Mags didn't care much for basketball yet. She would swing the big ball between her legs like her sister had taught her, and then sling the ball as high as she could, but she was still too little, and usually missed reaching the goal by two feet or more. Then, the ball would fly over the barbed-wire fence and into the soybean fields behind their property.

"Let's make mud pies," Mags suggested. "I'll go get some water. You find some good dirt to mix with."

The ground was mostly clay, good for mud pies. Lee Catherine positioned herself by the side of the house where there weren't any flowerbeds, but there was a small dirt pile left over from construction. An old stump would serve as the baking surface. Barney, their lovable, mixed-breed shepherd-collie, ran up to sit and watch. Barney was so big that Mags could ride his back like a horse, just like Lee Catherine used to. But soon, Mags would grow too big to ride Barney, just like Lee Catherine had.

Mags returned, lumbering along with a half-pail of well water. "Here," she said, setting it down with a splash. They poured water in the dirt pile and began to knead the mud like it was dough. They were careful to keep sticks and twigs out of the batter. Before long, they had patted out a couple of pretty substantial pies onto the top of the stump. The sun was out bright and spring was in full swing in Ferriday, Louisiana. It was 1968, and the Beatles had captured the children and Louise's fascination with their latest single "Lady Madonna." Not Daddy John's though. He still preferred country music. In fact, he broke the first Beatles' record they ever brought into the house. But that's another story.

It wouldn't take long for the pies to bake and harden in the sun. Later, they'd have a tea party and pretend to eat them. If their brothers got back from playing fort and war in the woods by the house, they'd invite them.

Mama called Lee Catherine and Mags in to eat mayonnaise sandwiches and leftover purple-hull peas for lunch. They washed it down with cherry Kool-Aid served up in red aluminum glasses, frosty cold. Louise also gave them each a small serving of leftover macaroni and cheese from a couple of days earlier. She made it with spaghetti noodles, cheddar cheese, milk and lots of black pepper, then baked it for about forty-five minutes. The cheese and milk would be bubbling hot when she pulled it out of the oven.

They ate at the bar overlooking the den and watched a Bugs Bunny cartoon on the television. It was quite a long distance from the bar to the television in the den, but the girls didn't seem to mind. Louise rinsed the dishes and suggested they go see about the progress of the mud pies, then do some weeding among the rose bushes and morning glories. Roses were Louise's favorite flowers. She doted on them and found solace in taking care of them, watching them grow, then breathing in their sweet fragrance when they bloomed. The experience made her think of great poetry and transported her to another place. She needed roses. She needed an escape. This was only one avenue she used. There were others.

Lee Catherine and Mags began pulling up weeds in the flowerbed in front of the front porch while Louise went to find her spade and hoe. She wanted to plant more morning glories so they would twine around the iron grillwork on the front steps. Sometimes, she'd watch them as they opened in the morning. Sweet life started anew, she would muse to herself.

As she made her way back from the pump house, she heard Lee Catherine yelp and Mags screaming, "Snake. It's a snake! M-a-a-a-ma! Hurry!"

Louise ran as fast as she could. "Stand back. Y'all just get away. Let me see if I can find it." She had a terrible fear of snakes. Before she married John and moved from the Mississippi side of the river to Ferriday, she had never in her life encountered one. They made her think of evil and death, and she hated them. Suddenly, she swung the hoe down hard, over and over, hacking away.

"I got it! I got it!" Louise yelled.

At that precise moment John drove up in his white Chevy truck. He saw Louise swinging the hoe and the girls cheering their mother on for her heroic efforts. John jumped out of the truck and ran to see what all the commotion was about. Louise stood proudly pointing at the dead snake. It was brownish-green and only about three feet long.

"Damn it all, Louise, what are you doing killing that snake," he demanded. "That's just an old garden snake. I've told you a hundred times not to kill the good ones."

"I couldn't tell for sure, and I wasn't going to take any chances," Louise said. "Are you sure that's not a rattlesnake?"

"No. It's not a rattler. Why can't you get it right, Louise? Why don't you ever listen to me and learn about these things? It's not that hard. See, a rattler would have markings on his body and he'd probably rattle too, if you'd stop long enough to listen instead of jumping to the wrong conclusion."

"Well, I guess the world's just going to come to an end, and all because I killed a good snake instead of a bad one, and by mistake, too. It's not like I did it on purpose." And tears began washing down Louise's face. "Why are you so critical, John? It was an honest mistake."

And with that, before he had a chance to say another word, Louise dropped her hoe and ran into the house so he wouldn't see her crying any more than was necessary. She had gotten to the point that she didn't want him to see how easily his disapproval could make her cry. She went into the bathroom off the front hall of the house and slammed the door and locked it.

John picked up the hoe and leaned it against the brick house that he had helped to build. His two daughters were staring at him.

"She didn't mean to do the wrong thing, Daddy," Lee Catherine said in the grown-up sounding voice she acquired when she was deadly serious. "She didn't. She thought the snake was bad and might bite Mags or me. She was only trying to protect us."

Mags' eyes had welled up as soon as her mother had started to cry and she began to sob loudly now. John picked her up and he reached for Lee Catherine's hand, but she crossed her arms and stared at him. "She didn't mean it to be wrong," she said bravely, with all the confidence she could muster, an eleven-year-old talking back to her daddy. "Mama wouldn't kill a snake if she knew for sure it wasn't poisonous."

John bent down with Mags holding him tight around his neck with her arms and around his chest with her pudgy legs.

"It's okay, Lee Catherine. You're right. Of course she didn't mean to. I'll go talk to her. Okay? I promise. In a minute. Let her calm down some first."

Mags stopped sobbing and pointed to the stump with the mud pies. They were dry and hard now, perfect for eating. They all kneeled by the stump and made-believe they were having tea and eating slices of chocolate pie. The boys ran up out of the woods. They were wielding sticks for guns and shouting at one another.

"Y'all stay out here and play a while. I'm going in to talk to your mother."

But John didn't get a chance to because Louise was walking out the front door then with a pitcher of Kool-Aid and several of the multicolored aluminum glasses on a tray.

"Y'all thirsty after your battle?" she yelled, as she set the tray on the front steps and began to pour.

Louise had washed her face and applied powder and some red lipstick. Her curly, auburn hair was brushed back and tied under, then on top in a bow with a blue ribbon that matched the blue specks in her eyes, which she turned to John who was staring at her.

"Y'all want some Kool-Aid?" she asked.

Louise had already, at least on the surface, gotten past the events of moments before. She was used to John's criticism. After all, they had been married for fifteen years. And maybe he was right. She probably went too quick for the snake, but why wasn't he here to help her? He knew she tried hard to learn what he tried to teach her, but she would always be a town girl at heart. Town girls, they just don't know snakes. That's all there is to it.

Lee Catherine looked at her mama and her daddy and all she could feel was love for these two confused grown-ups. She could tell they cared for each other a lot and she wanted them never to fight. But grown-ups always do.

To make everybody forget about the snake, Lee Catherine started telling her brothers and daddy the funny story about the lizards from that morning. Mags and Louise kept interrupting to add their versions, so they all told the story together. And before long, the boys and John were laughing in spite of themselves.

How-To Section

How to Bake Tofu: If you don't want to buy your tofu pre-baked, or your store doesn't offer it, you can bake your own. If you have a choice, buy the "firm" option. Preheat oven to 450 degrees. Open package and drain off water. Then gently put the tofu between sheets of something absorbent (I use paper towels.), and lightly press to remove excess water. Then cut into cubes, and bake on dry baking sheet for 40 minutes. At 20 minutes, flip the tofu over so you get even browning. (You may want to flip it more often.)

How to Make Almond Pie Crust: This recipe requires 2 cups of roasted almonds — see directions below for roasting almonds — 2 tablespoons raw granulated sugar, 1 cup powdered sugar and 1/3 cup sweet cream butter, plus 1 tablespoon to grease the pie plate. (Substitute soy or canola margarine instead of butter when making vegan version.)

First off, grind the roasted almonds in a coffee grinder or a blender. To prepare the crust, begin by greasing a pie plate with butter. Then pour 2 tablespoons of sugar into the greased pie plate and rotate the pan until it is completely coated with the sugar. Remove any excess sugar from the pie plate by turning it upside down over the sink.

In a medium glass bowl combine finely ground roasted almonds and powdered sugar. Mix them together well. Add softened butter and form into a kind of dough. Add the mixture to the pie plate, forming the crust as you go. It should look and perform just like a graham cracker crust. Bake the crust for 10 minutes at 350 degrees. Take crust out and let it cool for at least 45 minutes before adding the pie filling and baking pie.

How to Cook Rice: To cook rice, use a 2-to-1 water-to-rice ratio. So, for example, whether you are making white rice or brown rice and whether regular jasmine rice or basmati, you proceed as follows. Place 1 part rice and 2 parts water, (that is, 1 cup of rice and 2 cups of water), in a covered saucepan on high heat. Bring rice to a full boil, and then reduce heat to the lowest setting. Let rice cook for 30 to 45 minutes depending on amount of rice you are cooking. Best practices are to not let rice boil over, so you may want to watch lid after the rice boils and you turn the heat down, so you can remove the lid and then replace it if it starts to boil over. Also, you can tell if rice is fully steamed with no remaining water by sticking a fork in rice all the way to the bottom of the saucepan and moving it back and forth. It should feel dry on bottom, not mushy.

How to Roast Almonds: Almonds can be roasted on a large nonstick cookie sheet. Up to 2 cups of almonds will fit on a sheet. Simply place the almonds on a dry cookie sheet in 1 layer and roast them in the oven at 350 degrees for about 10 minutes. They should change in appearance from light brown to dark brown and may smell like cooking almonds. After 10 minutes, pull them out and set them on a rack or on top of the stove to cool. They may crackle and pop a bit in this process, but don't worry — it's all natural. Plain roasted almonds are a component of several of the pies in this book. They are also just great to make and put in a tin to eat at home. For a more festive or dressed up version, you can rub the cookie sheet with a little butter or coconut oil and top the almonds with brown sugar and cayenne!

How to Make Roux: Roux is the base for gravy not made from meat drippings. It is a component of several of my recipes in this book. You can make roux with butter or use margarine, if the recipe is vegan. Begin with ½ cup of whole-wheat pastry flour or rice flour, for glutenfree. Melt the butter or margarine until completely melted and hot. You can make roux in a skillet on the stove, if you want it to have a brown appearance or you can simply heat up the butter or margarine and add the flour. Stir in the flour little by little, avoiding creation of any lumps.

Little by little add the flour until the roux is of a pasty consistency. The amount of butter or margarine to make this happen can vary but should be around a quarter of a cup. Use roux to thicken stews and soups such as gumbo.

How to Roast Red Bell Peppers: Slice the red bell peppers in half length-wise and remove the seeds, the ribs and the top stem. In an oiled 6- to 9-inch skillet, place a peeled garlic clove under each red pepper half. Place the skillet in the oven at 375 degrees and let roast for 30 minutes or until peppers begin to turn black on top of skin. Take out peppers and garlic and set aside to cool. Please note, depending on how large your red peppers are, this step may require two skillets.

How to Rinse and Soak Beans: For a few recipes, the beans need to be sorted, rinsed and strained to remove excess water. After you finish this process, you want to soak the beans. Use a large stockpot or a large crockpot. Place the washed, strained beans in the pot, and fill to 1 inch from the top of the pot with cool water. Let the beans soak for 5 to 8 hours. After the beans are soaked, pour off the water and give them a quick rinse. Use the strainer again if that is easiest.

How to make Raw Macadamia Cream Cheese: Ingredients required: 2 cups macadamia nuts, 2 ½ cups filtered water, 2 tablespoons coconut oil and 3 probiotic capsules. Materials or tools you will need: cheese cloth or nut milk bag, a strainer, a really good food processor or blender, a mixing bowl, a measuring cup and a spatula.

Begin by placing nuts, coconut oil and 2 cups of water in a blender or a food processor. Blend until super-creamy. Open the probiotic capsules and dissolve into ½ cup of warm water. Pour the water/probiotics into the nuts and stir. Pour this mixture into the nut milk bag.

Twist the top of the bag and place into the strainer. Place a plate on top and add something heavy like a can of soup to press down the cheese. Allow it to sit in a warm, dry location for 24 hours. Remove it from the bag and place in fridge until chilled. Serve or use in recipes once chilled. Fresh and good to use for up to 9 days after chilling.

www.ingramcontent.com/pod-product-compliance
Lightning Source LLC
Chambersburg PA
CBHW050114170426
43198CB00014B/2576